61 Citizens

Terrorized by Kuklux

in & near

Alamance County, North Carolina, 1868–1870

as told in their own words & attested by others

in the

official transcript of the

impeachment trial

of

Governor William W. Holden

Numbers not including many children, spouses,
parents & acquaintances terrorized in said incidents

61 Citizens

Terrorized by Kuklux

in & near

Alamance County, North Carolina, 1868–1870

as told in their own words & attested by others

in the

official transcript of the

impeachment trial

of

Governor William W. Holden

edited & published by
a citizen of Alamance

*dedicated to four
who were unable to testify at
Governor Holden's impeachment trial
because on these dates they were
murdered by Kuklux*

Wyatt Outlaw *February 26, 1870*
William Puryear *a night in March 1870*
Robin Jacobs *May 12, 1870*
John W. Stephens *May 13, 1870*

*to the countless victims
whose names are not known*

Table of Contents

Introduction

*The first of eight charges against
Governor William W. Holden
in his impeachment trial:
he "corruptly and wickedly declared the
county of Alamance to be in 'insurrection.'"
The second charge:
he did the same in Caswell.*

Holden became governor twice in less than six tumultuous years before
his impeachment and removal from office in March 1871. He was ap-
pointed provisional governor in May 1865 by President Johnson, then
defeated in the first post-Civil War election by Jonathan Worth. In
1868 as the Reconstruction Acts restructured the state's government
in preparation of its return to the Union, Holden was elected in a land-
slide, with extensive support from African-American voters. Worth, who
especially resisted the idea of Negro suffrage that the Reconstruction Acts
guaranteed, at first refused to leave office, then said that he was leaving
"under Military duress" and "without legality."

After completing its new constitution in July 1868, North Carolina
with Holden as governor was re-admitted to the union; the subsequent
removal of military rule ended the protection that local citizens had
enjoyed. Within three months of taking office, Holden was hearing of
Kuklux violence throughout North Carolina. By that fall, violence and
threats had become worrisome enough that Holden issued an executive
order intended to protect all voting rights. In November 1868, in a pattern
that many whites found alarming, voters in some parts of North Carolina

elected candidates who were African American or sympathetic to their rights, and African Americans voted in large numbers. Attacks in those areas, such as Alamance and Caswell counties, increased soon after the election, and by early 1869 they were rampant.

Governor Holden persistently tried to protect citizens from these violent outrages. In April 1869 he issued an executive order prohibiting masked vigilantism and an appeal to all citizens of the state to join him in "discountenancing disorders and violence of all kinds, and in fostering and promoting confidence, peace and good-will among the whole people of the State." The attacks worsened. In eighteen months, he issued four proclamations, wrote to members of Congress and President Grant and to U.S. military officers asking for assistance with controlling the Kuklux, and authorized sending military officers and detectives into the afflicted areas to file detailed field reports. Finally he asked the legislature for the right to call a county in "insurrection" and to protect its citizens with state's military rule, and on January 29, 1870, the Shoffner Act gave him that power.

Meanwhile, the violent assaults continued. Wyatt Outlaw's murder at Graham, on February 26, 1870, finally brought Holden to declare, on March 7, 1870, Alamance in a state of insurrection, but it was July before the militia, led by the former Union guerilla leader George W. Kirk, restored safety to the areas. The Kirk-Holden War commenced on July 15, when Kirk began directing the arrest of local white men for, among other crimes, Outlaw's murder. Eighty-two were arrested in Alamance, nineteen in Caswell. Complaints over their treatment at the hands of militia would constitute five of the other six impeachment charges against Holden.

Holden's supporters suffered big losses in the August 1870 elections; later that month all those arrested by Kirk were released on judge's order, effectively ending the "war" although it wasn't officially terminated until November. Immediately after the election, conservative press began calls for Holden's impeachment, and after the new legislature was seated, it moved swiftly. Articles of impeachment were introduced on December 9 and adopted on December 19. Holden left his office on December 20; two days later, he and his wife were baptized.

To pay for his defense, which was led by Richard Badger, Edward Conigland, and J.M. McCorkle, Holden mortgaged his Raleigh home. The state provided for the prosecution, which was led by former governors William A. Graham and Thomas Bragg, who were also former congressmen; Augustus S. Merrimon, who had been a superior court judge since the end of the Civil War; and Thomas Sparrow.

The impeachment trial began in the senate chamber in Raleigh on January 23, 1871; on March 22, he was acquitted of the two most serious charges, that he had improperly declared insurrections in Alamance and Caswell counties, but convicted on the others, resulting in Tod Caldwell becoming governor and Holden leaving the state. A U.S. Senate committee investigating the reports of race violence in the South used some of the impeachment testimony but also documented extensively instances of similar Kuklux violence throughout the South. It also concluded in March 1871 that there were no serious problems between the races in the region. By March 1873, all alleged participants in vigilante assaults in North Carolina were pardoned and given amnesty from future prosecution. The Compromise of 1877 gave Rutherford B. Hayes the U.S. presidency, formally ended Reconstruction, and recognized "home-rule," or the individual states' rights to control their African-American population, with that power according to North Carolina's constitution generally enforced by county sheriffs.

LEONARD RIPPEY *white, 51 &*
JAKE BRANNOCK *colored*

Q. Give your name, age, and residence.

A. Leonard Rippey. 1819, September 9th, was my birthday.

Q. Where do you live?

A. In Alamance.

Q. Go on and state what you know of any outrage being committed on you, where you were, and all circumstances surrounding it without my putting separate questions.

A. I had some molasses that I had engaged to give my brother-in-law in Rockingham, and I was carrying the molasses to him on a one-horse wagon. Just as I got in the edge of Caswell County, seven or eight miles from my home, I came to a blacksmith's shop, and I wanted to get some work done on my wagon. It was Jake Brannock's. It was about one hour and a half by the sun when I got there. He could not do the work I wanted him to do on my wagon then, as he was doing work for a widow woman—her son was there having some work done on a wagon tire, cutting and putting it on, but he said as soon as he got through with that he would do my work. I held on to wait. When he got through it was pretty well night, and then I had some five miles to go to where my brother-in-law lived, and I was dubious about my making the trip with the wagon.

Mr. GRAHAM, prosecution. It is not worthwhile to go into all that.

Mr. MERRIMON, prosecution. Are you sure it was in Caswell?

A. Yes, sir, I am certain of that; I am well acquainted.

Q. Go on and tell what took place.

A. I had no cover on my wagon, and I asked him if I could stay that night by his fire.

Mr. GRAHAM. Whose house?

A. Jake Brannock's.

The CHIEF JUSTICE. He is a negro blacksmith?

A. Yes, sir, I laid down by the fire and went to sleep. By and by I heard a horn blowing and I supposed it was somebody around hunting. I then went off to sleep again. I waked up and I heard the horn blowing again. I still supposed it was some hunter around there but after a while there was a knock or calling out at the door. I sort of turned over. I was lying on my elbow like that [*illustrating*]. They called at the door but nobody made any move, nothing was said. The second time they called, Jake Brannock answered and called to know who was there. They said "John Spence," a yellow fellow; and then they asked him to open the door. Brannock says, "You cannot get in this house; who are you?"

They made no answer, but he opened the door, and said, "You cannot get in until you tell who you are"; and then I heard some rumbling beside the house. There was some wood on the side, and they took a stick of wood and begun to knock it against the door, and they came in right to me before the fire, where I was lying, and rubbed a pistol on my forehead, and told me to get up and go with them.

Q. How did they look?

A. They were disguised—had on white disguises that hung down pretty near their ankles and they were covered over their heads and had horns or something like that or ears. Of course I got up and they took me out of the house up the road some twenty yards from the door. They carried me on the road there and every now and then I passed some persons on either side with the same kind of clothes and horns until they got clear off two hundred yards. They then came up with Jake Brannock and they laid him down.

Q. Describe what was done.

A. They laid him on his belly, as well as I could tell, for they were all around, and went to whipping him. It seemed to me there were five or six whipping him at the time, just standing on each side and whipping him. He was lying on his belly when he laid down. I suppose he twisted around; I could not very well see.

Q. What did they do to you?

A. One of the disguised men stepped up to me and asked if I had a knife. I told him I had, he said for me to lend it to him. He discovered that I was considerably stirred up and he said, "You need not be uneasy, we are not going to pester you," but he went and cut some hickories and came back and handed me the knife. When they had got done whipping Jake Brannock they come to me and said, "We are going to give you twenty-nine, for being in a nigger house," and asked me why I had stopped in that nigger's house. They asked me why I did not go to some white man's house. I told them that I supposed I might have done so but I was there and I thought I might as well stop there; he then hit two licks and the other hit me three and told me to go back to the house.

Q. Describe the scourging that was inflicted on Jake Brannock.

A. They hit him a good many times—I cannot tell the number, there were a great many licks struck.

Q. What do you mean by a great many?

A. I would suppose that there were seventy-five or eighty lashes.

Q. State whether you saw him after he returned to the house.

A. Yes, sir; I saw him the next morning. He was very much hurt. I saw no part of his skin but his hands and a little up on his wrists. His hands were scarred and swelled up, and his face too.

Q. You did not see his back?

A. No, sir; I never saw his back at all. The night before, he helped me to put my molasses in his house, but he could not help me to take it out.

Q. Was anything said about politics?

A. There was one stepped up and rubbed his hand over my forehead and said, "You are a d----d old radical."

Q. Did you state when this was?

A. It was in November 1868, as well as I recollect.

Q. How many were there?

A. They looked to be eighteen or twenty.

Q. What has become of Jake Brannock?

A. I understand that he is somewhere up in Guilford over by Greensboro'.

…

SANDY SELLERS *colored*

Kuklux John W. Long testified about the whipping of Sandy Sellers.

Q. State whether you belonged to the organization called the Kuklux or White Brotherhood.

A. Yes, sir, I belonged to the organization known as the White Brotherhood.

Q. Look at that disguise. [A package was handed to the Witness, from which he drew a long white gown and a white head dress, covered with horns having red tassils at the ends, and coming down over the face, with openings for the mouth and eyes.]

Q. Mr. MERRIMON, prosecution. Suppose he puts it on.

Q. Mr. BADGER, defense. Put it on.

The WITNESS *then proceeded to attire himself in the gown and the head dress. [laughter]*

Q: I wish you to go on and state now, without being particularly questioned, as to when you joined this organization.

A. Well, sir, I joined at the Company's Shops in 1868, in Dr. John A. Moore's office. John T. Trollinger was chief of the camp I belonged to, and Jacob A. Long was the chief of the county as I understood it. The next meeting I was at was in a pine thicket near Anderson Thompson's. We met in the woods near Thomas Sellers' place. There were five or six men there when I got there, and there were two men there to be initiated that night. We initiated those men, and some of them proposed that John T. Trollinger, as chief of the camp, should come and go that night to whip Sandy Sellers. We went on to Joseph Hardin's where Sandy Sellers lived. We took him out of the house and went about three hundred yards in the woods and there tied him to a tree, took off his shirt and gave him two licks apiece.

Q. How many were there?

A. There were sixteen of us, I think.

Q. Why did they all whip?

A. Well, it was the order of the camp that we should all give him two licks apiece.

Q. Could you fix the time that was?

A. In 1868, it was near Christmas, I think.

Q. Go on. What next?

A. Well, we gave him a thrashing and went home and the next meeting I was at—

Q. Did you say anything to him after you thrashed him?

A. Well, we told him never to talk about white ladies the way he had, or something about some stock. The understanding was that the order came from Sheriff Murray's camp that he should be whipped.

Q. Go on and tell the next.

A. The next meeting I was at was between Company's Shops and—

Q. Wait; I want to ask if Sheriff Murray was the chief of a camp.

A. Yes, sir, he was chief of a camp at the time.

···

DANIEL WORTH *white*

Kuklux John W. Long testified about this incident.

Q. Tell all you know about Daniel Worth's school house.

A. Well, I was at work at Company's Shops and John T. Trollinger kept a bar room up close to Dr. John A. Moore's. I was going by their home, and he told me that he wanted me to come back there that night on some particular business. He wanted somebody that didn't have so much cowardice about them as others had. I goes up there that night and stayed there until about betwixt ten and eleven o'clock, I think, and he told me what he wanted then. We stayed there in the back room. I was not in the bar room.

Q. Tell what was said and done.

A. He said he wanted me to burn a house for them. As to whose house it was, he did not give me satisfaction that it was Daniel Worth's school at first. After a while he told me it was that, and I told him I didn't want to have anything to do with it. He told me I must—that it was an order from the camp.

Afterwards Thomas Gray got a jar of kerosene oil and a large syringe and we went on across the railroad to Priestly Ross's—Joe Ross's now—Priestly is dead. We went on down to the school house and Tom Gray told me he wanted me to be a watch. He goes over and takes the oil and squirts it all up on the ceiling and in the weather boarding and doors, and the balance of it down on the porch floor—a part of it on the bag that he had the oil wrapped up, and I said, "Mr. Gray, for God's sake don't burn that house." The first match went out.

He said, "I will burn it in defiance of Jesus Christ," and the second match he struck the house lit the oil and it took fire. We ran as fast as we could and the house was in flames.

We ran to John T. Trollinger's bar room and went in the back way and got in there. In a few moments they cried out fire and we went out to the fire.

Q. They cried out fire soon after you got in at the bar room?

A. Yes, sir.

Q. And you went to the fire?

A. Yes, sir.

Q. What did you do when you got to the fire?

A. We helped throw down the fence that stood there— standing in front of the house.

Q. Tell whether the house was burnt down or not.

A. Yes, sir. It was all burnt to ashes. There was a northern man kept school in the house by the name of Meader.

Q. Do you know why they burnt it?

A. That they had been keeping a negro school in there, and that this man had been teaching white children in the day time, and darkies at night.

Q. That is what Trollinger told you?

A. Yes, sir, and before that he said that Van Holt and Tom Gray had set the darkies' school house on fire, or made an attempt to set that on fire but it went out, that they would have burnt that had it not been that Van Holt ran—that he was such a coward that he would not stay there, but he was afraid to do the work.

...

JOSEPH HARVEY *colored*

Q. Where do you live?

A. Alamance County, Company's Shops.

Q. How old are you?

A. I could not tell my age exactly, some twenty-seven years old though, I reckon.

Q. Go on and state without my asking you any questions whether you have on any occasion met with disguised persons, and if so what they did, and all about it.

A. It was about two years I reckon as nigh as I can come to it, this March. They came to my house, I was sick at the time and I had got up. My wife had made me some tea, and I had got up to drink it. They bursted into my house—they took hold of me, I resisted against them a little but I found it wouldn't do any good—took me outside and tied me and carried me off about a mile and tied me around a tree and they all struck me five licks apiece first, and then they all struck me three licks around apiece.

Q. Had you clothes on?

A. No, sir, my clothes were off. I didn't have anything on but just my clothes I lay down in.

Q. Did they whip you on your bare back?

A. Yes, sir, they drawed me up over a limb and I didn't know anything—

Q. State how they drew you over the limb.

A. They just throwed the rope over the limb.

Q. After you left your house, state whether you heard any noise in the house.

A. I heard my wife holloaing mightily while they had me beside the house, she holload and tried to get out behind, she said.

Q. Don't tell anything what she said. You heard her holloa?

A. Yes, sir, I heard her holloaing.

Q. When did you return to your house?

A. I could not tell exactly the time it was when I got back but it was mighty late, they kept me out pretty late.

Q. Were you suffering a good deal when they were whipping you?

A. I was suffering a good deal, not any more than I had before or much more than other colored people who had been whipped.

They never put the rope around my neck not until they had taken me down there and whipped me. They tied my arms at the house. After they whipped me, one of them says, "Let us swing him up, maybe he will tell something." I told them that I had had a dispute with a white woman but as for saucing a white woman I never had done it. They said they were going to make me tell it. They tied a rope around my neck and drawed me over the limb.

Q. Did they pull you up?

A. Yes, sir.

Q. State how high—whether they pulled you off the ground or not?

A. Yes, sir, they pulled me off the ground, as long as I had my knowledge but they choked me soon.

Q. I understand you to say that when you came to, you found yourself on the ground and some of them doing what to you?

A. I found myself—or one of them had his hand on my breast here and said, "the d----d son of a b---h was just playing possum we will give him a little more," and he made me get up. I could not stand when I first got up; there were two of them stood, one on each side of me, and three of them struck me five more licks apiece around, and they would have killed me I believe, but one of them begged for me. They told me if I ever told it, they had not done anything to me to what they would do, and told me to go on home and say nothing about it. I went back home and my wife had left home and went down to my sister's.

They had struck my baby—five months old—right across the face here apparently—it looked like a blow. They all had clubs and it looked like a blow from the club they had. She said—

Q. Don't tell what she said—just describe if there were any wounds on the child and on your wife.

A. Well, they struck it across the face here, apparently, sort of smashed its nose, and the child never done any more good after that. It lived a few days after that and died—never cried like a natural child any more after that. There was not anything the matter with the child at that time.

Q. Did you notice any marks upon your wife when you went back?

A. Yes, sir. My wife had a scar on the side of her head here, where it looked like they had struck her with one of the clubs they had. My wife has never been well since, and has been complaining of her head ever since.

Q. I do not understand you in this respect. You did not tell how they got you out of the house. How did they get you out?

A. Well, sir, they just run in and gathered me.

Q. How did they come into the house?

A. They just bursted the door down.

Q. How did they carry you out?

A. Well, sir, they just gathered me and carried me right out.

Q. How did they gather you? We don't understand what you mean by gathering.

A. Well, sir, just fell over on me and gathered me and carried me right out.

Q. Do you mean they took hold of you or not?

A. Oh, yes, they took hold of me, I resisted against them a little, but I found it wouldn't do any good.

Q. You had been whipped before?

A. Yes, sir. On the breastworks they whipped me a good deal. I helped to throw up all the breastworks about here.

Q. What did they whip you for?

A. I run off once.

Q. How many times were you ever whipped in your life?

A. That is more than I can tell you.

Q. They hanged you up till you were senseless?

A. Yes, sir.

Q. How did you count the licks then?

A. I did not say they struck me when I was hanging up.

Q. No, but you said they struck you as soon as you were taken down.

A. No, I said they held me up awhile after they let me down.

Q. You were suffering then, and you could not stand up?

A. Yes, sir.

Q. Then it was that they said you were playing possum, and they whipped you again?

A. Yes, sir.

Q. How did you know that?
A. I came to myself.

Q. The first thing when you came to, you were counting?
A. No, I didn't say that.

Q. They whipped you though when you were coming to?
A. I said they held me up.

Q. Weren't you coming to when they held you up?
A. They held me up some time after I could not stand up.

Q. At what time did they put the licks on you?
A. Well, they struck me after I came to.

Q. You counted the licks?
A. Yes, sir, I did—that is, one stood off and counted.

Q. How do you know that anybody who was connected with whipping you struck your child?
A. I didn't say that I knew it.

Q. What did you say they did it for then?
A. I said the child had a bruise on it when I went back.

Q. Whether they gave the bruise or not, you don't know?
A. No, I can't say that. I know it had none when I left that night.

Q. Who struck your wife?
A. I could not say that.

Q. How do you know she was struck?
A. Because the bruises were on her when I came back. She showed them to me.

Q. Do you belong to the League?
A. I do.

...

MILLIE ALSTON *colored*

Q. How old are you?

A. I don't know my age, but as near as I can come to it I am near sixty.

Q. Where do you live?

A. In Alamance, on the other side of Haw River, on Greenmore's plantation.

Q. Did any disguised persons ever come to your house?

A. Yes, sir, about a year ago, just before harvest. The wheat was turning. They came and bursted open my door. I was lying asleep. Heard them, and I jumped up and was scared. When I jumped up there was one in white, or something going towards the door, and the other was coming around as I just sat up in bed, and after a while they came in the house, there were five of them, and one of them came to the bed with a pistol, and he pointed it at my breast. I said, "Please sir, don't kill me"—just so.

Then he took hold of my hand and pulled me off the bed, and he said, "Let us take her to the graveyard." One stooped down to catch hold of my leg. They afterwards said, "Let her alone," and began to whip me.

They never told me what they were whipping me for until after I was done whipped. There was four whipped me, one with a cedar switch, the other was a sweet gum, and another was a red elm, and they gave me twenty-five licks a piece and one of them stood by and counted the licks. The first one hit me twenty-five, and he stopped him, and then another, and he counted them in the same way. I was not thinking about the licks; I was trying to see what form they was in—to see what they was, as they was all dressed in white, and had great long robes down to the feet. I could only see red around the eyes and black around the mouth.

Q. State what clothes you had on.

A. I had on a new cotton frock. I had just laid across the bed; it was on Friday morning, and I had just laid across the bed, sort of tired.

Q. What time in the night was that?

A. I don't know exactly what time in the night, but when they left it was near about an hour and a half from day.

Q. How long did they remain there?

A. I don't know that they remained any longer than they got done whipping me.

Q. State whether you were injured by the whipping.

A. They welted me, and made me powerful sore. Just after they whipped me I washed myself in salt and water.

Q. How long did you suffer from the effects of that whipping?

A. I don't know. I reckon near about two weeks.

Q. Did you ever have anybody indicted about it?

A. No, sir.

Q. Why?

A. I didn't know the laws, and I didn't know nothing about it. I was scared, and I could not do anything with it.

Q. What did they whip you for?

A. I was living at Jim Newland's, in the yard, and I had a granddaughter that her mother left, and I raised her. She and some white children on the factory hill got into a tangle, and so Mrs. Newland—she did not like that—and she said she was going to whip her, and so she went out to the road and got a pine bush and she struck her with it. I was right by, and I gathered her and took the stick away from her. At that time, she halloaed and her girls came out and Henry Quackenbush told me to let go of the stick. I told him I would not, and he commenced beating me over the head, and he broke a green stick on my head twice.

Q. You had a fight right there?

A. Yes, sir, we had a hurrah there. After that I moved away from there.

Q. What did they say they whipped you for?

A. They told me, after they had done whipped me. One said, "Now strike a white woman, will you?" I was just scared and didn't know hardly what to say.

Q. How do you know they gave you a hundred licks?

A. One of them stood there and counted the licks.

Q. You say this white lady was beating your grand-daughter and you took this stick away from her?

A. Yes, sir, and I went and took the stick away.

Q. Did you say anything to the white woman?

A. If I did I don't know; she had hold of the stick and I had hold of it. We both had hold of the stick and one of the daughters went down to the store after her pa, and he came up there. We were both standing holding the stick. I was talking, and I said, "Miss Eliza Ann Newland, I think it is very hard for you to beat my little child on account of factory hill children; if it had been your children it would not have been so bad, but the factory hill children was nothing to you, and I think it is very hard."

Alston places her assault in "spring a year ago," which would have made it in 1870. Peter R. Harden, Alamance County justice of the peace, who testified to the U.S. Senate from notes he had made about assaults being reported to him, placed the date in early spring 1869.

...

CASWELL HOLT *colored, 36*

Q. Where do you live?

A. I live at Graham, Alamance.

Q. How long have you lived there?

A. I have been living there some over twelve months.

Q. Where did you live before?

A. I lived with Colonel Jerry Holt two years.

Q. Just tell what was done to you—all the circumstances, the first time; then the second time, and all about it; who came and how they were dressed.

A. One night I just lay down on the bed—I went up from Mr. Holt's. I was eating supper down there; he boarded me. I had four boys that worked with me about the house. They generally staid down at the house with him—

Q. Go on to the whipping.

A. I went home, lay down on the bed; the boys were there and they went down back to the house, and while I was lying there I heard some person come running around the house, and I thought it was the boys that had got scared and came back. I was lying on the bed. I said "Halloa."

They said "Halloa, is that you Caswell?"—just so.

"Yes, sir." By this time they were in the house—I hadn't the door fastened.

They said, "Come out here." Well, they gathered me by the arms and dragged me out of the bed, ran out doors with me, and commenced choking of me.

I says, "Men, don't choke me," —just so. I didn't think, you know, that they were going to hurt me, and one struck me—struck me in the eye; then I began to think they were going to hurt me.

They tied me then, and let me up. He says, "Come on here, go with me." I went with them on, I reckon, about three hundred yards from the house where I was, out into the woods. They then went out and came across a post oak tree that had a straight limb running out, and he says, "Now do you know how near your time?"

I says, "I don't sir."

"Well," he says, "this is your last moment."

"Well," says I, "if it is, I can't help it."

He says, "Do you recollect anything about them chickens now?"

I says, "I do not, sir."

He says, "Do you know anything about any wheat or corn?"

I says, "I don't sir,—just as I told you at first."

There was one then run up to the tree and threw the rope up over the tree, and says, "Draw him up"—just so—"draw him up." And they drew me up.

"There, let him down again." He says, "Do you recollect anything about it now?"

I says, "I don't, sir; just as I told you at first."

He says, "Well, draw him up again, it has got to come better than that."

They drew me up again and let me down.

He says, "Do you recollect now?"

I says, "No sir, I don't. If I have done anything or said anything, gentlemen, I wish you would please tell me, and if I have I will acknowledge and say that I did it."

He says, "That won't do, it must come better. Sit down here, G-d d--n you, sit down."

I sat down and they put my arms across my knees, as I sat down, and run a stick across through on both arms—bucked me, you know—then they all formed in a line before me; the one that talked, there was one that talked, he says, "Form a line, men, form a line around here," and all gave me three licks apiece, and they then let me up. "Do you recollect anything about it now?" he says.

I says, "I don't sir, just as I told you at first."

"Well," he says, "draw him up."

They drew me up again, and they took this stick that they had bucked me with and rubbed it up and down my back—one got at each end of it and rubbed it up and down my back. They let me down, then, and he said, "Now do you recollect anything about it?"

I said, "I don't, sir."

"Well," he said, "Who are you going to tell this to when you get away from here?"

I says, "I don't know sir, that I am going to tell any person."

He says, "You don't think you will tell this to any person?"

"No, sir," said I, "I don't."

"Well, d--n you, you won't for you won't get the chance of it."

"Well," said I, "If I don't get the chance of it, I can't tell it."

"Well," he says, "D--n you, you will swear that you won't tell it?"

I told him, "Yes, I reckoned I would swear that I wouldn't tell it."

He says, "You are to leave the county in ten days."

I says, "Gentlemen, I haven't done anything to leave the county for; I don't know why you should want me to leave it."

"Well, you have got to leave it now," he says. "Do you be off. I will give you that time to leave, and if you ain't gone we will be to see you in two weeks; and the next time we will kill you."

I went on then. He told me to be off now to the house. One run to me and gave me three licks after I started, and I went on into the house. I sent down for Mr. Holt.

Q. Which Holt?

A. Colonel Jerry Holt—my wife went after him.

Q. You cannot tell what she said.

A. And he came up and says, "Cas, what's the matter?"

"Well," I says, "a parcel of men came here and took me out and pretty nigh put me to death."

"What did they do that for?"

I says, "I couldn't tell you."

He says, "What did they say to you?"

"Well, sir, they questioned me about wheat and corn and chickens."

He says, "Who?"

"Well, I don't know," I says. "Do you know anything about any wheat or corn being stolen in the neighborhood?"

He says, "Yes, that is true. My son George has lost wheat and corn—"

Mr. GRAHAM, prosecution. I do not think it is worthwhile to go into this conversation.

Mr. BOYDEN, defense. I don't care anything about it.

Q. Where was the rope?

A. Around my neck, sir. They had cut my bed-cord and taken it and put it around my neck and threw it up over a limb.

Q. How far did they draw you? Did you stand flat on your feet, or on tiptoe?

A. No, sir, with tiptoe on the ground.

Q. How many times did they draw you up?

A. Three times, sir.

Q. In that way?

A. Yes, sir.

Q. Were you drawn up or not when they whipped you?

A. No, sir, I was sitting down when they whipped me— "bucked" down.

Q. You say you were drawn up at another time when they struck you with a stick?

A. They drew me up twice before they whipped me, and whipped me and drew me up again, and took the stick that I was bucked with and rubbed it up and down my back.

Q. On your naked back?

A. Yes, sir.

Q. State whether the bark was on the stick or not?

A. The bark was on the stick.

Q. You say two of them took hold of it and rubbed you?

A. Yes, sir.

Q. Describe more particularly this manner of bucking you, but first state whether they brought any blood or not.

A. Yes, sir.

Q. State how the bucking was done.

A. They took me and took my shirt and wrapped it all around my head. They had my arms tied this way [*showing*], and then I sat down on the ground and they put my arms over my knees and ran a stick through under here [*under the legs*] and over both arms.

Q. Over your arms and under your knees?

A. Yes, sir.

Q. And that doubled you up?

A. Yes, sir.

Q. Then they whipped you in that condition?

A. Yes, sir.

Q. What did they whip you with?

A. Whipped me with switches—some peach-tree switches and some cedar and some hickory.

Q. Did you bleed?

A. Blood ran all on the ground. My wife pulled a splinter out of my hip that long [*showing by his finger a measurement*]

Q. How long is that, two inches?

A. Yes, more than that.

Q. Did you say if they came out again you would be prepared for them?

A. I said this—

Q. I want you should answer my question.

A. I went to my old master that raised me—

Q. Answer my question whether you said it.

A. I can tell you the whole thing and then you can fix it just as you want it. I went to my old master that raised me to get him to advise me as to what was the best to do. He told me the best to do was to go along and say nothing about it, that I would find out a heap more about it than if I was to go and have them arrested, because these things, he said, had been existing in the northern states for many years, and that we men of the country could not understand them.

Q. I don't care about that.

A. I cannot tell you unless I tell you that.

Q. You can give an answer to my question.

A. No, sir, I cannot give you any unless I can tell you.

SENATOR ALLEN, juror. Mr. Chief Justice, I move that the witness be required to answer the question.

The CHIEF JUSTICE [to the witness]. You will answer the question the counsel puts to you directly.

Q. Did you not give it out that you were not ready the first time they came there, or something of that sort, but that you would be when they came again.

A. No, sir, I did not.

Q. Tell us how long you were confined.

A. Then I lay there some three or four days—four days—and after a while I began to feel uneasy, you know, about the time they said I was to leave. I got up and started down to the house. I saw [*Colonel Holt*] one day. I met him coming up to the house to see me.

Q. Did he see you?

A. Yes, sir.

Q. And saw your condition?

A. Yes, sir, he saw me that night after I was whipped, and I asked him what he thought that I had best do, leave or stay.

Q. State how badly you were whipped.

A. I was not able to work under three weeks from the whipping, to do any good. Well, it went on after I got able to work. I still continued on with him that year, until two weeks before Christmas—this last Christmas gone it was a year ago—they come one Saturday night; they come to the house and they asked me to open the door and I told them, "No, sir, I didn't open it unless they told me their business, what they wanted and who they were."

Well, they said, "G-d d--n you, open the door."

I says, "No sir, I won't do it." I had an ax sitting at the door, and one of my boys was there, and I went to reach him the ax, and I had a knife in this hand, and he says, again, "Open the door."

I says, "I shan't do it, sir."

One says, "Blow his brains out"—just so—"blow his brains out." As quick as he said that they all fired at the door, and they just shot me.

I clasped my hand in here, [*indicating the breast*] and said, "There, I am shot." And that boy of mine, he knew there were some loose planks in the floor, and he jerked up two of those planks, and all my family run under the house except my three little children and myself. They took rails and bursted in the door.

He says, "What are you doing with this knife?"

I says, "I had it sir,"—and he jerked it out of my hand and put it here to my breast and then said, "G-d d--n you, I have a mind to run you through your d----d heart."

Another says, "Let him alone, he is shot."

"He isn't shot," he says.

"He is shot," said the other, and he jerked open my shirt bosom, and says, "There, you see, he is shot."

He says, "Oh, yes."

Then he said, "G-d d--n you, you said you was not afraid of any Kuklux in the county."

I says, "I didn't say that, sir. If you heard that you heard it from somebody else besides me. I didn't say it."

He says, "Are you afraid of them now?"

I says, "I have got nothing to do with you, sir."

He says, "Do you know me?"

I says, "I don't, sir, I don't know anything about you."

He says, "Where are all those boys of yours you had here?"

I says, "I don't know where they are; they are gone, I reckon. They were here a few minutes ago."

One of them says, "I will be G-d d----d if we don't burn them under that house." Another says, "No, throw the things out," and they threw the things out. Another says, "Come, George, we must make quick time here," and from that they were all gone, and I haven't seen anything more of them."

The next morning I sent for Dr. Montgomery to come see me, and he came and took out the bullets, and that evening they moved me to Graham, and I have been there ever since.

Q. How many shot hit you?

A. Well, sir, there were two balls went into this arm right here [*indicating right arm*]—there were three shots in that arm, and two balls here in the right side, and one shot right in there [*indicating about the region of the lungs*] and one ball there [*the left side*].

Q. Were you ever troubled except on those two occasions?

A. No, sir.

Q. These men came there and began to enquire about chickens and wheat and corn, you say; did they not tell you that they were going to whip you for stealing?

A. No, sir, they just asked me about those things.

Q. Did you not tell Colonel Jerry Holt that they said they had whipped you for stealing?

A. No, sir, I told him just what I have told you now.

Q. Did you not tell Jerry Hold that they said they had whipped you for stealing?

A. No, sir, I told him just what I told you about wheat and corn and chickens.

Q. Did you not tell him that they said they whipped you for stealing?

A. No, sir, they did not tell me that they whipped me for stealing, they asked about chickens and corn and wheat.

Q. I am not asking what they said, I am asking what you told Colonel Jerry Holt.

A. I only told him what I have told you and I asked him if he knew of any person who had wheat or corn missing in the neighborhood anywhere and he said he did, that his son George had. I said that was the wheat and corn that I was questioned about that night—just so.

Q. What did you mean by that?

A. What I meant was that they asked me about wheat and corn.

Q. That George Holt had lost wheat and corn?

A. Yes, sir.

Q. How did you know it was George Holt's wheat and corn they questioned you about?

A. That is all he said he knew of. I did not know of any other.

Q. Did they say that night that they whipped you for your behaving indecently to white women?

A. No, sir.

Q. They did not charge you with exposing your person to a white woman?

A. No, sir, they never said anything about that.

Caswell Holt testified that his first assault occurred "about three years ago," which would have placed the event in March 1868, prior to any reported assaults; Peter R. Harden, the Alamance County justice of the peace who testified to the U.S. Senate from notes he had made about assaults being reported to him, said that the first assault on Holt occurred in early spring 1869.

...

JOSEPH McADAMS *white, 49*

Q. Go on and state what you know about any secret political organizations in that county.

A. I don't know much about it; there was a parcel of men put a coffin at my door.

Mr. GRAHAM, prosecution. Mr. Chief Justice, we object to this testimony. What has this to do with the question whether there was insurrection in the county of Alamance? It appears to me that it has no relation whatever with the issue that is now pending.

Mr. McCORKLE, defense. Mr. Chief Justice, it shows the lawless character of the people.

Mr. GRAHAM. It has no bearing whatever on the question of whether there was an insurrection, they might just as well be allowed to prove that a carcass of a dead animal or some equally offensive thing has been placed in this witness's yard to annoy him.

Mr. SMITH. Is it not an outrage to put a coffin at a man's door? It is quite evident of a threat of death, it may be of the man, and if that is not a criminal act which with other outrages goes to show the necessity of declaring the country in a state of insurrection, I don't know.

The CHIEF JUSTICE. The presiding officer is of the opinion that the evidence is competent upon the ground that it is a fact which may have a bearing upon the issue before the court.

Q. State what you found at the door.

A. It was a regular made coffin. It was set up against my door, and before the door. I heard a noise when the coffin was put against the door. The dogs attacked some of them, and I immediately afterwards got up and commenced opening the door, and the coffin commenced looking in; I did not know what it was; I thought it was a plank or something, at first. I opened the door a little further, and took my foot and kicked it off and I think the top fell off.

Q. Was there anything in it?

A. No, sir.

Q. Any writing on it?

A. Yes, sir. Lengthwise there was these words, "Hold your tongue or this will be your home." Crosswise it said, "Alive to-day, but dead to-morrow. KKK!" I then went out and hitched my dogs, and there were four or five guns fired about sixty yards apparently from the house.

Q. When did you say this was?

A. The 20th of April, 1869.

...

JOHN BASON *white*

Q. Where do you reside?

A. I reside in Alamance County, two miles from Graham. I have been living there on and off for twelve years.

Q. What office do you hold there?

A. Postmaster, at Haw River.

Q. Go on and state whether you know of any disguised persons visiting you and when it was.

A. Sometime in 1869, it was either the latter part of August or the first of September—it was in very warm weather—I went to the depot—the train comes in about ten o'clock at night as near as I recollect now—to get the mail. The depot sits about three or four hundred yards from where I live. I went and got the mail and came on back and opened it and gave out the letters to all the persons who were there. They had all left and I went out to the store piazza. It was quite warm. I was then guarding Mr. Holt's factory.

Q. Whose factory?

A. Thomas M. Holt's. I sat down on the store porch and staid there I reckon a quarter of an hour, or it may have been longer, and I saw a man coming towards the well, but he was not disguised at the time. He went on under the hill and I staid there a few minutes, and then afterwards the thought struck me that it might be somebody who was going to the factory to do some mischief, so I went to the factory and walked about the factory from under the hill. I could not see anybody at all. I then walked up to Mr. Holt's office and walked a few steps and sat down on the door steps right by the door. I had been sitting there some fifteen or twenty minutes when I saw seven or eight disguised men dash in each end of the store piazza and they run over the chair where I was sitting on the piazza before I left, and they made a right smart fuss. They found I was not there, and they dashed into the counting room of the store where Mr. Williamson was sleeping. They staid in there I reckon a minute, perhaps a little longer, and they came out of there and came running under the hill to where I was sitting in the office until they got to within fifteen steps of me. I got up and they halted. Two of them just dropped in, two abreast, side by side, one with a four-shooter and the other with a long knife which looked as if it was twelve or fifteen inches long, with a blade about an inch and a half wide, which looked as if it had been made in a blacksmith's shop. When they came pretty close to me, I spoke to them and asked them what they wanted. They did not make me any answer. I asked them what I had done and they failed to answer me; then they gave a sort of a grunt like a hog when he gets scared.

Then they walked in front, and the balance behind. I asked what they wanted, and what I had done? They made no answer at all, but they kept sauntering around. They didn't take hold of me the first time a right smart bit, but they sauntered until one got one side and the other the other, and another man caught me by the arm, and another by my feet, and jerked my feet from under me. I live the furthest house from there, and I could see the folks looking down the road to see what was going on, and I halloaed, thinking that they would come to my relief. I reckon we scuffled fifteen minutes on the floor, until I got so warm that I was nearly exhausted. I told them that it they would let me alone I would get up and go with them if they wanted me; that I had done nothing, and was not afraid to go with them anywhere.

I tried to prevail on them not to tie me, but they tied me pretty severe.

Q. How?

A. In this way [*showing his wrists crossed.*] One man took me, and a part of them kept away, as they were afraid I would know them I reckon. They tied me and took me down the road they came. They took me down to the railroad between a half and three quarters of a mile when they came to where there was a branch running through a field under the railroad. They took me down in the hollow, and threw a rope over a limb. There were a good many cedar bushes, and they gave me I suppose three or four licks a piece, but it didn't hurt me except one. One hit me two licks. I think he did it with a cedar limb, and that hurt me pretty bad. He struck me on the legs. I asked them if they were satisfied, and they made no answer, and they told me to go home, and said that if I said anything about it they would be certain to come back and take my life.

Q. You say that there had been a great many outrages perpetrated and that nobody could be convicted?

A. There were so many that I thought it best to let the matter alone.

. . .

JOHN ALLRED *white, 42*

Q. Where do you reside?

A. About eight miles south of Graham, in Alamance County.

Q. Go on and state whether you were ever visited at night by disguised men, &c., and what did they do to you.

A. There was a parcel of men came to my house one Saturday night, the last fall a year ago, I think it was September.

Q. September 1869?

A. Yes, sir.

Q. What time in the night?

A. Betwixt twelve and one o'clock. I was asleep and was waked up by a powerful noise—a tremendous noise—and I soon found out that it was the Kuklux, or I thought so, and I told my wife to get up and tell them I was not at home. So I lay still and she got up and through a light broke out of the window they talked to her and she answered them—a parcel of foolish talk, as I thought.

Q. Just state what occurred between them.

A. They asked her where I was, she told them I was gone over to Alamance Creek. Well, he said he liked a woman that would tell the truth, for he was a woman himself.

The CHIEF JUSTICE. What was said?

The WITNESS. My wife said I was gone over to Alamance, and he says, "That is in New York, where we come from," and says he, "I like a woman that will tell the truth for I am a woman myself." Then he said, "What is your husband's name?"

"Allred," she says.

"Well," he says, "you tell him when he comes home that if he don't change his politics and be a white man we will cut his

throat next Saturday night," or "make his throat red"—I don't
recollect which—I didn't understand that, directly, but it was
one or the other. Then they went "Kukluck! Kukluck!"—off
down the road.

Q. What did they say when they went off?
A. "Kukluck! Kukluck!"

...

JOHN SHATTERLY *white*

Q. What is your age?

A. I don't know my age exactly, but I am some thirty years old.

Q. State whether you were visited by persons under peculiar circumstances, and if so, state all about it.

A. In October 1869, if I am not mistaken, a band of men came to my house in the night and shot into my house—towards my house. My dog was barking, and I was awake, and I got up and was standing in the door as they came down the road. My house is close to the road. As soon as they shot I snatched my gun which was over my door. I asked three times who was there and nobody spoke, they began to crawl down by the fence.

They squatted down around. It was tolerably dark. But as many as I could discover was two. They stood right up by the fence after the others squatted down.

Q. How were they dressed?

A. They had spotted concerns on as well as I could tell— white and black.

Q. What do you mean by concerns, had they ladies' dresses on, or clothes?

A. It was a kind of concern which is called disguising, I suppose.

The CHIEF JUSTICE. What was done?

A. Well, sir, I shot in among them, and I heard one begin to groan as though he was hurt. I heard one ask him something, I did not understand what, and he holloaed out "I can't," and he repeated again "I can't."

I stepped back in the house to load my gun in time, and they put back up the road where they came, but I concluded that I had better watch, as they might come back. I stepped out between the kitchen and the smoke house, and I heard somebody walk up the path back of us. I watched pretty close until I could begin to see a glimpse of him, when I cocked my gun. My wife commenced calling in the meantime, "Don't shoot unless they come into the yard."

I said, "Halt you good-for-nothing scoundrel—you have come within one of getting killed, and that should be a warning, and you had better stay away or I will kill you." He scrambled on back towards the hill there was behind, and I heard him everlastingly make the weeds pop in running.

Q. What time was that?

A. My clock was not running, but I suppose it was between one and two o'clock.

Q. Were you one of them who acted as Kirk's pilot?

A. I went with him to a few places.

Q. Were you the one who furnished names to Kirk for his men to go around and take people?

A. I told him some few names, I believe.

...

WILLIAM LONG *colored, 31*

Q. Where did you live, and what was your occupation?

A. My trade was shoemaking, and I lived on Mr. Daniel Tickle's land.

Q. State whether you were whipped, and if so, under what circumstances, tell all about it?

A. In October 1869, I was employed by Mr. Louis Tickle to make his family some shoes—to go to his house and make shoes. Finally on Monday morning I got my tools and I went there and worked until Wednesday. On Wednesday night, after supper, everything was over, and I went to work again on my shoes by candle-light. After eight o'clock—it was not nine, but it was nearly about bed time—one of the daughters went out of the door, and she came back excited, so much so that she could not tell me what was the matter; in fact, she did not have time, but in the course of a few minutes the door was clustered with about eight or ten disguised men.

Q. How were they disguised?

A. They had on white robes coming over the head bound with red and with horns on, some straight and some turned down, as I experience. Then they called for a negro. I did not say anything. Mr. Tickle got up and he asked what they wanted, he said they wanted me, he said let him alone that he was not doing any harm, they finally insisted that he should come out, and that I had to come out. He told them to go back and behave themselves, that he did not want any foolishness; then they told him that they were not going to trouble him, but all they wanted was the negro. He looked back and said, "Bill, you will have to go." I had a shoe knife in my hand and was just trimming the bottom and they ordered me to put down the shoe knife. I did not want to go and was slow to do so but I went to the door and they laid hold of me and they wound me up so [*illustrating*]. I did not try to get loose; in fact I was afraid to undertake it.

Q. Did they have any arms?

A. One had a sword and others had clubs. They took me about a quarter of a mile I reckon, to a place I was very well acquainted with, for I had passed it for years. There was a post oak tree that had double prongs growing up from the root. I had noticed it many a day. They concluded they would hang me up. Finally, some says not—I suppose they did it just for a sham. They asked me if I knew anything about breaking open a house.

I told them "No, sir."

He says, "Don't say you don't."

Q. Whose house?

A. He said, "Don't you know anything about the breaking open of Daniel Patton's house?"

I said, "I did not." I said, "When was it done?"

He said, "Between eight and ten months before."

I said, "I was in Salisbury at that time."

He said, "No, I was not."

I said, "I was."

He said I was not, "you tell something about it."

I said, "I am willing to tell anything that I know but I don't know." Finally they untied me the way they had me and then tied me again sufficient to stretch my arms across and bucked me—you all know what that means, I suppose. They took down my clothes—they did not take off anything but they tore my clothes.

He said, "I want you to tell me something about breaking open that house."

I said, "I have nothing to tell you."

He said, "You have got to tell something."

I said, "I have nothing to tell, I don't know."

And they whipped me a while and then asked me questions and would whip me again and asked more questions.

I grunted very loud and they commenced whipping me again.

"Now," he said, "what have you got to say?"

I said, "Gentlemen, what must I say?"

The captain—I supposed it was the captain—gave notice to commence on me, and they gave it to me pretty strong. Then I took the heaviest portion of the whipping. Then he said, "Now what have you got to say?"

I said, "I will say anything you want me to say, I don't care what it is."

Then he drew a pistol and he said, "It has got to come out whether you did."

I was rather trembling and I could hardly move and I said, "What must I say?"

He said, "I want you to say whether you broke open that house or not."

I said, "I will acknowledge to everything you say," and I asked them when the house was broken open and whether anything was taken and they told me when the house was broken open and I repeated that over and finally whose house it was and when it was done and what was taken. I knew nothing about it but whatever they said I was to acknowledge I did. I was trembling and I said that I did everything that they told me because I was trying to save myself and was ready to say anything, I did not care what it was.

Then the captain stopped and gave orders not to give me anymore. He used a little partiality towards me—a little kindness or favor and then he asked me all about the farms there was about there and the condition of the farms and the corn crops. Then they asked me how I got into the house, whether I broke the lock. I told them I got in the window. Then they went behind the tree and laughed a little. They knew I was not telling a straight story, and they told me I had better leave the county. I told them that I had done nothing to leave the county for. Then they asked me all about stealing. I told them just as they had said because I wanted to get shut of the punishment. I told them I did not want to leave the county, that I had done nothing to leave it for, that I had been true to the county and had been friendly to all my neighbors and I did not want to leave my neighbors. Finally they gave consent to let me go back to Mr. Tickle's—that is all I know.

Q. You were not tied when they whipped you?

A. Yes, sir. My wrists were tied that way [*showing the wrists crossed*], then they threw me down, put my arms over my legs and ran a stick through.

Q. That is what is called "bucking"?

A. Yes, sir. I was never treated so in my life. I never committed offense against the civil law that I recollect, and have never been whipped by a white man except when I was small to make me mind.

Q. Do you know how many licks they gave you?

A. That is a hard question for me to answer. I will give you my best understanding. I will say between seventy-five and eighty. If a man says less than seventy-five, my back will contradict it.

Q. Was it severe?

A. It was severe as the man could put it on; and they didn't put it on in different places but they put it on the same place.

Q. Were there many scars on your back—many scabs?

A. There was some few scars where they whipped me in a different place, but most of the whipping was done in one place. There was no skin left. There was a place in my back where you could lay a grain of corn, after it became corrupt.

Q. How long did you stop work after that whipping?

A. If you will allow me to go back I will state. That was on a Saturday night, and I had a pair of shoes which I had bound when I had left to go to Mr. Louis Tickle's to work. It would not do to stop there in the condition in which I was, but I made out to put the bottoms on those shoes, which was about four hours' work for me. Had to do that and carry them home and get the money. I then came back and fixed myself and walked to Jim Sellers', the colored minister. There I finally gave out and stayed there until Saturday morning, and I got up and then went to Graham the next day, and I was laid up for two weeks before I was fit to get a job or undertake to make arrangements for myself.

Q. What kind of laugh was this they gave?

A. A laugh as if they were telling a little story or something. They had all clustered around behind the tree. They didn't say anything that I could hear, but rather whispered.

Q. Were you ever prosecuted about that alleged stealing?

A. I never knew anything about it. I never knew of this house being broken open before they prosecuted me for it.

Q. Did you have anything to do with Daniel Patton's house?

A. It was like a dream to me. I never heard of it.

Q. Why did you not have them indicted?

A. I was thankful to get out of their clutches and I concluded I would say nothing about it. They told me not to do so. They told me if I did, I could not get shut of them anymore. I told them that if ever I did they might kill me. He said, "I will not ask you to do that, but if you do we will do it any how."

Q. How long did you remain in that neighborhood?

A. I only remained in that neighborhood one day after it was done.

...

ANDREW SHOFFNER *colored & his wife*

Q. Where do you live?

A. Guilford County.

Q. How far from the Alamance line?

A. About a mile

Q. How old are you?

A. If I live to see the middle of this month I shall be sixty-six years old.

Q, State whether you have seen any Kuklux or disguised persons, and if so when.

A. I have seen them and felt them, too. They came out of Alamance to my home.

Q. How do you know they came out of Alamance?

A. I knew their voices and I was familiar with their manner.

Q. Tell when this occurrence took place, how many there were, and all about it.

A. There were seven, but I don't know the day when it was. It was about ten or eleven o'clock.

Q. How did they come into your house?

A. They broke the door down and took me out and whipped me.

Q. Tell all about it.

A. They took me out of bed and whipped me.

Q. How did they come into your house?

A. They broke down the door and came in and took me out in the yard and whipped me.

Q. Tell how they took you out.

A. They caught me by the heels and dragged me out of bed on my back. After they got me to the door, they caught me by the arms and put me on my feet.

Q. Did they carry you off in the woods?

A. No, sir, just outside of the door. Just clear of the step, that was all.

Q. What clothes did you have on?

A. Just my drawers, and they took them down.

Q. What sort of a whipping did they give you?

A. They whipped me—I think they gave me about fifty licks. It was laid on pretty well—not light.

Q. Was the skin cut?

A. Yes, sir, they cut the skin in several places.

Q. What did they whip you with?

A. It was a hickory. It looked like a shaved stick. I looked at it after they let me loose. After they found that I knew them or thought that I knew them, they went back and turned around their backs towards me to keep me from looking at them. I think that was what they did it for.

Q. What did they do after they got through whipping you?

A. They come and got my wife out of bed. They caught her around the arms and lifted her out.

Q. What clothing did she have on?

A. She had on a chemise.

Q. Did you see them whip her?

A. Yes, sir.

Q. How many licks did they strike her?

A. I reckon they struck her twenty or thirty; but they did not hit her hard.

Q. After they got through whipping her what did they do?

A. They went into the house and made a light, and went and got my gun, and took it down the road a piece and struck it against a tree and broke it to pieces.

Q. How did you know these persons—they were disguised, were they not?

A. Yes, sir. By their voices. They were boys raised right by me, not more than a mile from there.

Q. What did they whip you for?

A. Just because I voted the radical ticket.

Q. How do you know?

A. They told me so before that they would show me how to be a man.

Q. You didn't tell when they whipped you.

A. It was the 27th of last gone October a year ago.

Q. Did they whip your wife for voting in the election too?

A. They whipped her for being a midwife.

Q. Is there an objection to that profession?

A. They had an objection to it on account of Dr. Coble.

Q. She came in competition with Dr. Coble?

A. Yes, sir. She had a good many cases that he would have got if she had not been there. She was that much lower than he was, and she got them.

Q. They said that was what they whipped her for that night?

A. They didn't say it that night; they said it before that night.

Q. They were going to stop her practice?

A. Yes, sir.

Q. And your voting?

A. Yes, sir.

Q. Who said that they whipped her on account of her interfering with Dr. Coble's practice?

A. A neighbor woman not more than half a mile off told us that; she was a white woman.

Q. What she said has nothing to do with this. Did any of them say in your hearing that that was what they whipped your wife for?

A. They said no more than that they would learn her not to go where she had no business.

...

ALONZO B. CORLISS *white & his wife*

Q. State whether you were employed at any time in the last year or two as a school teacher in North Carolina.

A. I was, in Alamance County, at Mebansville and Company's Shops.

Q. Were you visited by any men in disguise?

A. On the evening of the 26th of November 1869, I preached to the colored people at their request, during a revival which they had; there were some noises about the window during the evening; I went home.

At twelve o'clock at night something was thrown on the roof of the house which waked myself and my wife, and then a rail came against the door and broke the lock; in came five men; I was rising from my bed; two of them seized me by my legs and dragged me out of the door; soon two others took me by the arms, and four of them in that way carried me in double-quick time about a mile and a half and set me down in a thicket and began to beat me with hickory sticks; I felt relief then, for I thought they were not going to hang me; I felt three blows; the next day revealed thirty marks on my back; I have the scars now. I fainted; the first I knew they kicked me in the side and said, "Get up," I rose part way and fell back; they lifted me up, and one of them shaved my hair close, one-half of it, and with a sponge painted half of my face black; the smell of the turpentine revived me; they then started to go away; I said, "Friends, will you tell me if I am near any house?"

One of them came back and said, "This way is the road;" I could not walk; they took me without my crutches. I took a stick and hopped along till I came to the house; my wife was out screaming for me up the road. I ought to have stated that they struck her; she tried to tear the mask from the face of one of them; I have got the mustache that she tore away from his face; they struck her on the arms and stepped on her feet.

Q. How were they disguised?

A. With tight clothing, something like a clown with horns. They whistled all the time, trying to appear like demons. Before they whipped me they stood around in a circle and gave unearthly shrieks and whistled. They went at word of command; they seemed to understand their business. While they were carrying me they said they meant to rule this country.

I asked them why they did this to me?

They said "for teaching niggers and making them like white men." They said they came from Chatham County. My knee was callous; I have a callous joint. They pulled it out straight and I screamed. They told me to hush up, we were passing a house, or they would blow my brains out, and they struck me with a revolver over my eye-lid.

Q. Had you taken any other part in the proceedings in the state or county?

A. None at all, except when colored men bought land and paid for it, and did not get any deed, they would come to me for advice; and I told them to pay no money until they got the deed; not to pay part and have a promise. I was trying at the time to have a free school system in operation for white children and for black children, also. I talked about it with leading men. The Friends had one school for whites and one for colored in Company's Shops.

Q. What became of your school house?

A. Well, they came around it that night. It had been disturbed by noises; the colored people said there were disguised men about it; I did not pay much attention to that.

Q. How long did you teach at that school?

A. At Company's Shops I taught six months, and at Mebansville one year, making thirteen months in all in Alamance County.

Q. How were you supported?

A. By the Friends of Philadelphia in part; the colored people themselves paid on an average $8 a month toward the school.

Q. Was it in consequence of this state of things that you left there?

A. It was; I could not stay there; my family would be disturbed all the while.

Corliss never returned to North Carolina; his testimony is from the 1871 U.S. Senate report.

Kuklux Dr. John A. Moore testified in the Holden impeachment trial about examining Corliss the morning after he was whipped:

Q. Tell what you found.

A. I found him pretty tolerably badly whipped, with a gash over—I am not certain whether it was his right or left eye. I closed that with a sticking plaster and I dressed his back. His back was not cut, but I could see the bloody water oozing through in several places, and he was complaining some of his lame leg.

Q. He was a lame man?

A. Yes, sir, he had had a white swelling I think, in time.

Q. Did you see Mrs. Corliss?

A. Yes, sir. She said that she had been hit. She complained of her being struck over the head, or something.

Gideon L. Gleason also testified at the Holden impeachment trial about the event:

The first that I knew that anything was going on in town I was alarmed by his wife coming to my gate and halloaing—halloaing murder. I jumped up and ran out to the gate and met her.

Q. This was at the Company's Shops, was it?

A. Yes, sir.

Q. Plenty of men there, were there not?

A. I suppose there were fifty men maybe more in that town.

Q. Were there screams loud enough to rouse the town there?

A. What, of his wife? Pretty loud—as loud as she could hallow.

Q. And nobody came out did you say?

A. I did not see anybody out.

Q. You did not offer to raise any of them to go after these men or go yourself?

A. No, sir, I went back in the house.

Q. You say you helped Corliss that night?

A. About a half an hour after his wife halloaed at my house. I heard somebody halloaing at the gate and calling me by my name. He seemed to groan some and called me out there. I went out to the gate and it was Corliss. He asked me there to—

The CHIEF JUSTICE. Don't say anything what he said.

A. At his request I took him in to the fire in the basement story of my house. I had a black man there with me who was a carpenter. I told him to go out and bring a blanket and put it over him. He was cold and minus his clothes excepting his night shirt. I hung the blanket over him, took him to the fire in the basement part of my house where the black man was sleeping that night. I thought he was somewhat exhausted and I got some brandy or whiskey, I forget which, and gave him some and then sent the black man down to his wife and she came and got him and the black man went back with them down to her house.

Q. Did he complain much?

A. He complained that he had been whipped. He complained right smart and I didn't see any part of anything except his legs and his arms, and you may say his head. He had this blanket on him.

Q. How about his head?

A. From one side of that the hair was taken off. It looked like it was done with scissors and was blacked. He looked like he had been blacked, had had it rubbed over his face. He was bout one half black and one half white. One leg I think was black, as well as I recollect.

Albert Johnson, white, 58, also testified at the Holden impeachment about this event:

I occupied a room at the Shops in the north corner of the hotel—immediately fronting the north. About one o'clock I heard an alarm and I went to my window and heard a female voice screaming like a maniac and calling my name and asking me to get up. She said that the K.K.'s had taken her husband off.

Mr. GRAHAM, prosecution. You need not state what she said.

Q. What did you do?

A. I put aside the curtain to my own room in the window in a condition to be able to see out, and could hear her voice. I told her to come around to the door. She came around and in a few minutes I put on my clothes and I heard her halloaing murder and that the Kuklux had got her husband and was going to kill him. She halloaed all over the village in different localities.

Q. What was her condition?

A. Her face was bloody all over; she was in a loose gown thrown over her very carelessly and she said they had struck—

Mr. GRAHAM. Do not speak of her conversation.

•••

CARTER CASSEY *colored, 55*

Q. Tell all you know about the matter of your chastisement— being whipped, who did it, when it was, how many there were and whether they were disguised or not.

A. I don't know who it was did it.

Q. Tell all that took place.

A. Oh, I was badly whipped.

Q. Tell about their coming there, where they found you and all about it.

A. Well, they come in one night at the dead hour in the night. I was laying down asleep and they took a rail and just come and jobbed the door—bursted the door off and pitched right into the bed on top of me and gathered me and took me out—took me out to the railroad and they all had sticks and beat me with the sticks.

Q. How much did they beat you?

A. Beat me about an hour I believe—that is my judgment [*laughter*]—it appeared like it was longer than that. My shirt was just as red as a red flannel shirt. They beat me on the head and shoulders and then stamped me on my breast with their shoe heels—stamped me on the breast and back.

Q. How many were there do you think?

A. There were five took me out of the house, and they said there were five more. They told me there were ten in the crowd.

Q. When was it?

A. Last year—last fall was a year.

Q. What did they whip you for?

A. I told them that I hadn't done anything.

Q. What did they say they whipped you for?

A. They said we'll let you know we are going around and whip all old radicals, and we know you are one.

Q. They didn't tell you that they whipped you for killing Lewis Gerringer's sheep?

A. They asked me if I hadn't stole it; I told them no. They asked me if I was accused of stealing it; I told them I didn't know whether I was or not, but they said I was an old radical.

Q. Didn't you say they whipped you for stealing George Tickle's pigs?

A. No, sir, I didn't either. [*laughter*]

Q. You say they took your gun and knocked you down?

A. Yes, sir. They almost killed me when they whipped me. They had a gun and knocked me down with it and beat me.

Q. Knocked you senseless?

A. Yes, sir. Knocked me down with the gun and I lay there and they beat me, I don't know how long.

Q. Were you out of your senses?

A. Yes, sir.

...

JAMES COLE *colored, 21*

Q. Go on and state whether any persons disguised ever came to you.

A. I was pestered by them—I was whipped.

Q. Where did they find you?

A. They found me at home in bed with my wife. They came and opened the door and they came in and took me out and then two of them held out my arms by my hands and the rest of them whipped me.

Q. State what clothing you had on.

A. I had on a woolen yarn shirt and a pair of black Kentucky jeans breeches.

Q. Where did they take you?

A. There in my yard. They gave me about thirty licks and then they told me that if they had to come back any more they would hang me.

Q. How were they disguised?

A. They had on white pants and then a white body buttoned around here—like little boys. Then they had a face with horns on each side—here.

Q. Were their faces covered?

A. All but holes for the eyes and mouth.

Q. What did they whip you with?

A. Hickories.

Q. What was the nature of the whipping?

A. There was one man hurt me very much—the first man. The rest didn't hurt me so bad, but it was very severe—all of it.

Q. How many licks did the first man give you?
A. He gave me ten licks.

Q. How many other men whipped you?
A. I don't know.

Q. Are you satisfied you got as many as thirty licks?
A. Yes, sir.

Q. What did they say they whipped you for?
A. They said they whipped me for keeping a girl.

Q. Did you keep the girl?
A. I did.

Q. Did that bring about a disturbance in your family?
A. No, sir.

Q. Did you and your wife get along smoothly together?
A. Yes, sir.

Q. Did your wife know about it?
A. I expect she had some idea of it.

Q. Did your wife complain about it?
A. No, sir, I stopped it before she had time to grumble.
[*laughter*]

Q. Did you keep any other woman but that one?
A. No, sir.

Q. Was she a married woman?
A. No, sir.

Q. Did she have any children?
A. She had one.

Q. Black or white?
A. White.

Q. Was it your child?
A. No, sir.

Q. Did you feed her?
A. No, sir.

Q. Didn't you give her corn?
A. No, sir.

Mr. BOYDEN, defense. I think, Mr. Chief Justice, that it is improper to go into such evidence—to ask such questions as have been just propounded.

Mr. MERRIMON, prosecution. We intend to impeach this witness—that is our purpose.

Mr. BOYDEN. But I would like to know how it impeaches a witness to know whether he had given a woman any corn.

...

PETER MEBANE *colored*

Q. Will you state whether at any time you have been whipped by disguised me?

A. Yes, sir. They were dressed in white. They took a rail and bursted down the door and come in. I was lying in bed and they took me about a quarter of a mile from home as near as I can come of it.

Q. When did you say?

A. Last fall was a year ago.

Q. State what they did to you.

A. They just took me out of the house and took me way down the back road, about a quarter of a mile as near as I can come at it. They pulled off my shirt and breeches and made me sit down in the road, and they all stood around me and they all whipped me.

Q. Pulled off your shirt?

A. Yes sir, stripped me right stark naked, and they stood all around—just had me in a ring.

Q. What else did you have on then?

A. They stripped me stark naked. They made me sit down in the road.

Q. You say they took your pants off?

A. Yes, sir.

Q. Entirely naked?

A. Yes, sir.

Q. You sat down in the road?

A. Yes, and they all stood around—just had me in a ring.

Q. How many licks were struck you?

A. Well, I was scared pretty bad; it seemed like they gave me about three hundred as near as I could count, I could not tell how many they gave me, I was scared so.

Q. What were you whipped with?

A. Hickories.

Q. How severe were the blows?

A. I was hit pretty bad, it seemed like—

Q. Was your skin cut?

A. Yes, sir. They cut the blood out of my back.

Q. What did they say to you, that they had whipped you for?

A. They never said a word only they just told me to go back home. They were all standing in the road, and I started back home.

Q. It was because you belonged to the Union League?

A. Yes, sir.

Q. Did you belong to it?

A. Yes, sir.

Q. Did you make any complaint to a justice of the peace or anybody?

A. No, sir. The boss—the man I was working with, told me not to say anything about it.

Q Were you able to work afterwards as you had?

A. I did not go to work for three days.

Q. Not able to work?

A. No, sir.

Q. Were you ever whipped before?

A. No, sir, never in my life as long as I can remember.

William McAdam, white, testified about the incident with Mebane.

Q. How long had he been whipped when you saw him?

A. I saw him then next morning after he was whipped.

Q. When was that?

A. I think it was in the fall of 1869.

Q. What was his condition, and how was he whipped?

A. He was badly whipped. His back was cut all over. Deep gashes in his back, deep enough to lay your finger in I noticed.

Q. Was the skin cut at all in other parts?

A. Yes, sir, it was cut in several places.

Q. Do you know how long he was disabled from work?

A. He was not of much account for three, four or five days. He worked with me.

Q. Where did he live at the time he was whipped?

A. He lived on my place, about a quarter mile off.

Q. You didn't know at the time the whipping occurred?

A. No, sir, I didn't know anything about it at the time. His wife came running to my house squalling in the night.

Q. How long have you known this man?

A. Ever since he was a small boy.

Q. Do you know what his character is?

A. His character is good, as far as I know. His old master gave him a good recommendation. He was a great deal better than common, and that is one reason I took him in.

Q. A good character for what?

A. For honesty and industry.

• • •

HENRY HOLT *colored, 33*

There are two men named Henry Holt in this narrative, the one who testifies here, referred to in the transcript as "Henry Holt, no. 2," and the one alluded to later in testimony by Mary Holt, who was married to the other Henry Holt.

Q. Go on and state what you know about disguised men going about.

A. I saw some this last gone fall twelve months ago. There was a parcel of men came to my house, and called out, and told me to come out. I told them I would as soon as I could put on my clothes. I was putting on my clothes, and they told me if didn't make haste they would put five hundred balls through the door.

I told them, "Gentlemen, if I have done anything to put five hundred balls through you will have to put them through"—just so. I said that.

They burst the door open, and three men came in with pistols drawn, and told me to make up a light and do it quick. I made up a light. They said they come from Greensboro', and they had to go back to Greensboro' that night, and said they were there by authority to settle that—that I had been cursing white folks and they wanted me to settle it.

I told them I hadn't, that I had never done such a thing.

They said I had, and that I must not dispute white folks' words.

I told them that I could not help denying it, because I never had.

They said I had—they knew I had. They said they had come from Greensboro' that night to settle it. I told them that I had not cursed any white people, that there was a good many people in that neighborhood knew me ever since I was born, and that I had never been in the habit of cursing anybody.

One of them said I must not talk so; if I did he would shoot me and one of them ran up and shot a pistol off right over my shoulder by the side of my head. By that time they had gathered around me and said, "Be still," and ordered me to hush talking. One of them said, "Take off your shirt."

I did take it off.

Then they marched up around me. At that, they gathered around me. I could not tell how many licks they struck me. I think they gave me thirteen or fourteen licks. I did not pay much attention to it. I don't know but more than that.

Q. How many were there in your family?

A. Nobody but my wife and two little children.

Q. What did they do to your wife?

A. They struck her a couple of licks, she said. I did not see them.

Q. You don't know what they struck her with?

A. No, sir, nothing more than a hickory.

Seymour P. Holt, white, a magistrate, also testified about Holt's treatment.

Q. Do you know Henry Holt?

A. Yes, sir, I know Henry Holt, a yellow boy, who was examined here the other day.

Q. Do you know of his being whipped at any time?

A Yes, sir.

Q. Did you examine him?

A. I examined his right arm only.

Q. How much was he whipped?

A. There were several welts on his arm—raised bruises, streaks.

Q. Was he complaining of his condition?

A. Yes, sir, he complained of being pretty badly whipped.

Q. Was he working with you?

A. He was not working directly with me. He was living on my land. I raised him, and he had been living there ever since his freedom. I had him as a tenant.

Q. Do you know what his character is among those who know him?

A. His character is as good as any man of his color in this state, I reckon, a man of truth and honesty.

Q. Have you known him from childhood?

A. I have known him ever since he was born.

...

SAMUEL GARRISON *colored*

Q. How old are you?

A. I do not know my age.

Q. Where do you live?

A. Alamance.

Q. How long have you been living there?

A. I was bred and born there.

Q. Go on and state whether you have ever seen any person disguised.

A. Yes, sir. They had on white gowns coming away down about the knee, that come over their bodies and heads, and great long ears like a mule's ears, about that long [*illustrating*].

They came and bursted open the door. I did not know they were there until they bursted open the door, and I jumped up. I was aiming to get out of the door, but they met me, and caught me, and struck me several licks on my head with a club, and from that they caught me, and threw me down and began to tie me and choke me. I told them not to choke me so hard. They tied me and took me a mile from away down the creek in widow Sally Faucett's field. They took me up the creek and made up a fire, and they started to tie me to a big Spanish oak, and did so, but I slipped the rope off my hand and I started to run but there was a little sapling behind that caught me, and they bucked me down. They pulled my shirt out of the drawers, and they whipped me first on one side, and then on the other.

Q. While you were lying down?

A. Yes, sir, first on one side, and then on the other.

Q. I thought you said they tied you to a tree?

A. They did first off, and then when I tried to get away they tied me down and bucked me.

Q. How long were you laid up through the whipping they gave you?

A. About two weeks.

Q. Tell the court about this bucking.

A. They squatted me down and tied my hands together and put my arms over my knees and put a stick through or between my legs and arms. [*illustrating*]

Q. What was the nature of the whipping, severe or light?

A. Severe. They cut my skin badly. The wounds are on me now.

Q. State whether they were indicted for this outrage on you?

A. Yes, sir, I went to Yanceyville on account of it.

Q. But this was in Alamance.

A. Yes, sir, I went to Yanceyville, and then came down to Company's Shops on account of it.

Q. But were these men indicted in the courts of Alamance County at Graham?

A. No, sir, I have never been to Graham about it.

Q. Why did you not go to Graham to have them indicted?

A. I was afraid to go.

Q. You were afraid?

Mr. GRAHAM, prosecution. We think this is not competent. The law gives its protection to everybody in this country and it is no excuse to a man that he was afraid. It is very well settled in this state than any man in any community who has been injured, as this man says he was, need not be afraid if he desires to seek the condemnation and punishment of those who have committed an outrage upon his rights. This attempt to excuse delay is not tolerated in law at all.

Mr. McCORKLE, defense. Mr. Chief Justice, the suggestion is remarkable. Here is a set of men embracing hundreds of the citizens of a county who are banded together to commit crime and intimidate a large portion of the people of the country, and counsel gravely suggest that it is a contempt of court for a witness to say that he will not apply to that kind of people for redress. To have done so would have asked for bread and got a stone. Had he sought for legal redress, he might well have feared another whipping at the hands of the men he persecuted. That was one of the very reasons why the county was declared in a state of insurrection. The people were intimidated by the violence committed upon many of the citizens and they dared not go to the courts.

Mr. BADGER, defense. Mr. Chief Justice, the argument would apply very well to a peaceful and intelligent white community and to intelligent white citizens, who knew their rights. But to attempt to apply any such rule to the case of a poor ignorant colored man like this witness is farcical. Such was the condition of affairs that he dared not apply to the courts.

The CHIEF JUSTICE. The presiding officer thinks the evidence is competent as tending to prove one of the allegations in the answer, to wit: that the county was in such a condition that the people were afraid to apply to the magistrates, and that they dared not deal out justice.

Q. Did you state what clothing you had on when they carried you off?
A. I had only on a shirt, drawers and was barefooted and bareheaded.

Q. What sort of weather was it?
A. It was a powerful cold night.

Q. How far did they carry you?
A. About a mile from home.

Q. Who constituted your family?

A. There was my wife and four children—five children, one of them has since died.

Q. Whom did you leave there?

A. I didn't leave anybody. They left home when they took me off from them.

Q. Where did they stay that night?

A. When I came back I found they were gone from home—I went to a neighbor's house, a colored man's, and they were not there; then I went to another house—I went to Mr. Allred's—they had gone to his house. I went and got them and came back home, and then we were still afraid and we went and stayed at a laboring man's that night.

Q. How did you happen to know these men?

A. I knew Asa Isley, because he had two fingers off. He had no gloves on, and he whipped me and cut hickories left handed.

Q. How did you know [John Rich] Ireland?

A. By the gown floating over his burnt ear.

Q. He was a deputy sheriff then?

A. Yes, sir, I think he was.

Q. Had you ever been whipped before that?

A. No, sir.

The CHIEF JUSTICE. You have never been whipped since you were free?

A. No, sir, I never was whipped for doing any crime.

David Allred, white, 52, testified about seeing Garrison after his whipping.

Q. Will you state whether you saw his wounds after he had been whipped?

A. On Monday morning I went to his house in the tan yard. He had been working at the tan yard, and I went over there. He asked me to go and look at his back. He wanted to have some tallow from the tan yard to grease his back. I then went with him over to the house. He stripped off his shirt and his wife washed his back and helped grease it. He seemed to be cut very bad. He seemed to have been cut on one side and then on the other side. I didn't see how the hickory could have struck on both sides, but it seemed to be on one side and on the other, half way up his back and down to his hips, along across his hips. It didn't seem to be marked right in the middle of the back. Well, I never saw many folks whipped, though I have been south and seen some whipped. But I never saw any as bad whipping as that was. I have seen some whipped at the public whipping post, but I never saw such a whipping as that was. I have seen white and black both whipped, but I don't think I ever saw anybody cut quite as bad before.

Q. How long was he laid up?

A. I think about two weeks that he did not do anything. He seemed very stiff when he went to work—so that he couldn't roll a wheelbarrow about the tan yard.

Q. Are you acquainted with the character of Samuel Garrison?

A. Well, I think it is as good as any black man's. I heard nothing said against him of any importance at all.

...

WILLIAM F. SIMPSON *white*

Q. Will you state your name, your age and residence?

A. William F. Simpson. I was born in 1819, the 13th day of March. I was born and raised in Alamance County and have been living there ever since till from last March the 16th to about the first days of September.

Q. Go on and state whether you have ever seen any persons riding at night disguised, and under what circumstances?

A. I never seen none riding, sir. I saw some come to my house, though. They came there on Saturday night. There was no person there except me and my two children. My wife was gone from home. They made a fuss and roused me up, and I don't think I answered the first time that I heard the fuss; but about the second time I heard it I answered, and got up immediately and opened the door. I was so nigh asleep I couldn't tell which door they were at till I got up and opened it. I got up and opened the one nearest that was to me; that was the south door, and when I opened the door I didn't see nobody. I just stepped out. I stepped around the corner—

Q. What kind of weather was it?

The CHIEF JUSTICE. Let him go on and tell all about it.

A. It was clear. I stepped around the corner, like, to my left hand, two or three steps from the corner, I reckon, and just about the time I got around so that I could see the north part of the house, they came around both sides of the house at the same time and ran right up to me and caught hold of me, one by each arm. In a few moments—it was only a moment or two—they got hold of me by each arm, and had my arms stretched out so [*illustrating*], and got hold of my shoulder and wrist. The largest man—I always called him "that big one"—he motioned to go and started out; there were some persimmon trees in the field, just out of the yard a little bit, and they started towards those persimmon trees. The ground was sown with wheat, and it was very spongy. I said, "Gentlemen, don't go out there; that ground is wet." He turned and came right down the road; kept down the road to where there was an inclosure; went down through the brush where there had been some little undergrowth cut down—down to a quarter of a mile from the house, and led me up to a black jack tree, the two that had hold of my arms. I says to them, said I, "Gentlemen, why do you treat me in this kind of style?" Says I, "I haven't stole nothing. I am no roguish man and I am no man that touches anybody if they let me alone."

That biggest one says, "You are in the habit of drinking and cursing and abusing a certain party."

"Well," says I, "I will admit that I say more at election time than is necessary," and says I, "I ain't alone, excuse me."

Says he, "What are you doing with that old nigger on your land?"

"Well," says I, "he was without a home and he put a pitiful mouth to me and I let him move in the house."

He says, "You must put him away."

I says, "I will try."

He says, "You must not say you will try; you must say you will in ten days." And then he pulled my shirt out of my drawers and stuck it up under my collar, and they whispered around a little around the tree and came and struck me about—

Q. Had you been tied?

A. Yes, sir. I had been tied; the tree was about large enough for my arms to reach around it that way [*illustrating with his arms*]. They whispered around and struck me about fifteen or twenty licks. I intended to holler when they commenced whipping me. I attempted to do so and he caught me around my face here and made a blood-blister on my lip, and said,

"You must not holler, sir." When he had struck me fifteen or twenty licks, one of them that had hold of my arms and tied me, says, "Give him about twenty-five more," [*the witness here spoke in a nasal tone of voice*] but he only struck me four or five more.

The CHIEF JUSTICE. Do you mean to say that is the tone of voice he talked in?

A. Yes, sir; I told him, "If you will talk with me in your proper voice maybe I can answer you." They came and poked their faces around my face and said "ha! ha! ha!" [*in a flat tone*].

Q. State whether you were injured by this scourging?

A. I was injured in several places, they brought the blood out of my back—whipped me with a hickory wythe and the next morning I went down there and found splinters an inch or an inch and a half long sticking into the bark of that tree, where I was.

Q. Did you state what kind of tree it was?

A. It was a black jack.

Q. You say they told that one of the reasons for whipping you, besides your talking about a certain party, was that you had permitted a negro to live on you land?

A. Yes, sir.

Q. State how long you had leased to him the land.

A. Till new year's; he did leave, but he didn't leave in ten days. I told him next morning, said I, "Jim, I want you to leave here," and told him the nature of the case and the treatment I had.

Q. What was the name of that colored man?

A. He used to belong to old John Shaw, and then Morton bought him.

Q. What was his name?

A. They sometimes call him Jim Shaw and sometimes Jim Morton.

Q. What sort of man was Jim Shaw?

A. He was a black man.

Q. What was his reputation?

A. Some said he was as nice a nigger as anybody, and some said he was a roguish nigger. That is all I know about it.

Q. You were in the army?

A. Yes, sir, and I had six brothers in, and every one of them was a good soldier too,—besides me.

Q. The Confederate army?

A. Yes, sir, there was no run and no disguise about them.

...

JACK PATILLO *colored, &*
IVISON WARREN *colored*

Andrew Murray, white, testified about these two assaults.

Q. Proceed and state what you know about outrages, if any, and where.

A. Sometime in December—about the last of December 1869, there was a party I saw. That night a negro woman that lived near my house or rather a tenant, came to my house and woke me up to come and relieve her husband—a party of men had him killing him. I went and she told me that they were in the direction of another tenant's that lived a little further on—about a quarter of a mile off. I took my gun and went, and when I got nearer this farthest house there was a tremendous fuss, beating and holloaing. I met, before I got to the house, this tenant's wife, saying that they would kill her husband.

Mr. MERRIMON, prosecution. You need not state what she said.

Q. Who was the tenant?
A. Jack Patillo.

Q. I understood you to say you heard this disguised crowd say that they intended to shoot you?
A. Intended to kill me.

Q. Will you state why you did not make yourself known to the crowd?

Mr. GRAHAM. Let him state only what occurred. His reasoning on the subject is a matter of no importance.

Q. You had your gun there, standing off from the crowd in the dark?

A. Yes, sir.

Q. You did not go up to them?

A. No, sir.

Q. Did I understand you to say that a house had been pulled down?

A. Yes, sir; about a month previous to that the house this man Patillo lived in was thrown down by some parties, I do not know whom. I had raised it on Friday and Saturday, and that Saturday night it was thrown down and there was a gallows created close by with six vines—grape vines—attached to it, and just a little off there were graves marked off, six graves with a rock at the head of each, as tombstones, and a notice stuck up, "No more building to go up, or you will be dealt with by the K.K."

Q. How long before this whipping occurred did the building of his new house take place?

A. About a month. He moved into the new house on Thursday, and Saturday night he was whipped.

Q. What is the character of those negroes whipped?

A. Well, sir, this man Patillo, I never heard anything laid against him. He lived with me twelve months previous to the whipping, and the family that raised him said there was nothing against him in this county.

Q. When you got there, what did you see?

A. Well, when I got just opposite the house on the hill I saw a party of men, seven or eight in number, dressed in white with lanterns. I got to this house, some hundred yards behind where they were. I went down in a hollow and they were up on the hill. They were whipping another colored man that they had taken first, and I got—

Q. What is his name?

A. His name is Ivison Warren. I walked within about forty or fifty steps of the parties to ascertain what they would do. By the time I got that distance they ceased whipping and they commenced questioning. They asked if I was going to protect them. One of the boys replied, "as far as was right."

Q. Which one of the boys was that?

A. Ivison, the one they were whipping. Then they asked them where were the arms that I had given them to protect themselves. The reply was that I had never given then any.

Q. This was a conversation you overheard?

A. Yes, sir; I didn't make it known that I was there. "Well," says he, "d--n him, tell him we are going to kill him," and then they made the negro pray for them, and then the crowd broke up.

Q. State whether you examined the backs of the persons of these two colored men, after they had been whipped.

A. I did. The one that they had then, that they had just whipped—I don't think they whipped him very badly. He was perfectly naked when he came to me after they let him loose. His skin was cut some.

Q. How about the other one?

A. I went back to my house and found the other one at my house.

Q. You mean Jack?

A. Yes, sir, Jack Patillo.

Q. You say he was badly beaten?

A. He was very badly beaten—so much so that I went for a physician. I did not think he would live. In fact, he was not able to sit up with the fright and the wounds, and he was suffering greatly. His head was cut very badly, and he was bleeding all over his face.

...

GEORGE RIPPEY *colored, 50*

Joseph E. Holt, 68, white, testified about Rippey being whipped.

Q. Do you know a man by the name of George Rippey?
A. Yes, sir.

Q. Is he white or colored?
A. Colored.

Q. Do you know anything of his being whipped?
A. Yes, sir. I used to own the boy, and when the United States troops came to Graham the boy did not live in the neighborhood. They all got free and he came to the company that was stationed there to report himself. He had been whipped and he sent for me, as I lived in the town and was his old master, to see him examined and to have justice done him. He did not know how to act.

Q. How old a boy was he?
A. He was about fifty.

Q. Did you see his back?
A. Yes, sir. He was badly bruised up—whipped up. He was whipped with a lash—with a strap.

Q. Could you form any idea of how many licks were given him?
A. I could not; only he was very wonderfully bruised up.

Q. Whereabouts?
A. All across his back. He had been struck terribly.

Q. Was he complaining much of the injury?
A. Yes, sir, he was complaining a good deal.

Q. Of severe pain?
A. Yes, sir.

Q. What has become of him?

A. He is dead.

Q. How long did he live after that?

A. He lived two or three months, I suppose.

Q. Was he ever well after this whipping?

A. He never was.

Q. Do you know whether he was laid up and had to go to bed after the whipping?

A. Yes, sir. He was laid up. All across his shoulders and back where he was bruised up by welts it had raised up in a puff and broke and run.

Q. How long had you owned this man?

A. Several years.

Q. What was his character?

A. He was a bidable good boy and first rate servant.

Q. And remained so up to the time of his being free?

A. Yes, sir.

Q. He was respectful to white people?

A. Yes, sir.

Q. Not impudent nor saucy?

A. No, sir, he was a good boy and first rate servant.

...

JOHN GUY *colored, 45*

Q. Will you state whether, on any occasion, and if so state the time and place you were visited by disguised men, and how many there were of them, and what they did—tell all the facts.

A. In the first place, there were twenty-five in the company, I believe, but I do not know how many licks they hit me.

Q. When was it you saw them?

A. I forget exactly what time it was.

Q. Can't you come near to it—was it this year or the previous?

A. It was the same night that Porter Dixon was whipped.

Q. Do you mean Porter Mebane—is he the same as Porter Dixon?

A. I never heard him called that. He was always called Porter Dixon.

Q. Where were you?

A. I was staying down at my Uncle Bill's.

Q. They came into the house before they whipped you, didn't they?

A. Yes, sir.

Q. How did they get into the house?

A. They opened the door and let them in.

Q. Then what?

A. They took me out.

Q. They just ordered you out?

A. They led me out. They carried me about three hundred yards, I reckon, from the house, not far from the big road, close to Mr. White's, out in the edge of an old field.

Q. Did they do anything with you before they whipped you?

A. No, sir.

Q. They whipped you with your clothes on?

A. They took my clothes off.

Q. You pulled your clothes off?

A. Yes, sir.

Q. What clothes did you pull off?

A. I took off all I had on.

Q. Did you do that yourself, or were you ordered to do it?

A. I was ordered to do it.

Q. I want to know what they did to you.

A. That is all I can tell about it. I do not know exactly how many there was whipped me.

Q. How many licks did you get?

A. I cannot tell.

Q. How many were engaged in whipping you?

A. I do not know how many whipped me. There was so many standing around that I didn't take no notice how many whipped me.

Q. What were you whipped with?

A. They had switches.

Q. What sort of switches?

A. I cannot tell what sort. They had wooden switches, I reckon.

Q. Were you whipped a little or badly whipped, or how?

A. I was whipped very bad. I was scarred pretty bad, all around the shoulders and down to my hips.

Q. Have you been whipped at any other time since that?

A. Yes, sir, I have been whipped since that time, something about a month after the first time. They came to my house, and took me out and whipped me. I think there was ten or twelve in that company.

Q. Where were you that night?

A. I was at home. They broke the door open. They took me out. They tied my arms in this way [*putting his arms behind his back*]. They took me off and made me strip and they whipped me, and they hit me eighty licks.

Q. Who was present with you?

A. I have no one but my children.

Q. No wife?

A. No, sir.

Q. How old is your eldest child?

A. The oldest I believe is going on sixteen.

Q. How many have you got?

A. I have three.

Q. How did they come into the house?

A. They broke the door open.

Q. What did they do with you then?

A. They took me out.

Q. How do you know there were eighty licks?

A. The man counted and I paid attention while he was counting them.

Q. Counted them out loud?

A. Yes, sir—counted them out.

Q. While you were struck?

A. He would not let but one whip at a time—that was when he counted.

Q. How many licks did you get from each one?

A. There was ten I think whipped me.

Q. What else did they do?

A. When they got done whipping me, they tied me to a tree.

Q. With your back or your face to the tree?

A. The back. After they tied me, they went away.

Q. How did you get out of that position?

A. Two of them came back and untied me.

Q. Why did they whip you?

A. They said I told of another man that I suspicioned him being a Kuklux. The first time because I had married a white woman.

Q. Did they say you were a white man?

A. They said not.

Q. Are you understood to be a colored man?

A. Yes, sir.

Q. Were you always treated as such?

A. Yes, sir.

Q. And you married a white woman?

A. Yes, sir.

Q. When was that?

A. Three years ago.

Q. I thought you said you did not have a wife when they came?

A. They parted her and me.

Q. Were you married before a magistrate?

A. It was a preacher, I believe. His name was preacher Beale.

Q. Did you get a license from the court?

A. Yes, sir.

Q. Where at?

A. Graham.

Q. Were you indicted in court for it?

A. No, sir.

Q. Never?

A. No, sir, no indictment only that night. That is the only indictment I got.

Q. Did they charge you with stealing?

A. No, sir, they did not charge me with stealing.

Q. You were asked whether you were a colored or a white man. Were your father and mother white or colored?

A. They were colored.

Q. Was your mother as white as you are?

A. Yes, sir, I reckon she was. I think if anything she was whiter.

Mr. GRAHAM, prosecution: The Guys have always been regarded as colored people up there.

Mr. BOYDEN, defense: This witness is certainly beyond the limit. It is very apparent that he is a white man.

Q. Which party do you belong to?

A. I belong to the radical party.

…

NED STROWD *colored*

Q. Go on and state whether any outrage was committed on you in the county of Alamance.

A. Yes, sir, just two weeks before Christmas a year ago— three weeks before Christmas a year ago, I was living at Mr. William Thompson's. I done all his hauling and driving a wagon for him, and he was taken down very sick, got out of his head, and his brothers expected him to die and had taken the business out of his hands and took it into the hands of themselves, and sold out his horses and things, and turned and rented the land out to other common white people.

But he got well before they got the business fixed to take the land. And then he preserved off a lot for me again to still stay with him and still work for him and drive his wagon and wait upon him. There were four white people living on the place—four besides me—that had rented the land. He moved me then to his house and told me where my ground was that I should have, and preserved me off a horse and handed it to me to work. I goes then and sows some wheat in a lot he gave me. I didn't have but a little to sow and sowed it in a little lot. Mr. Lasley come along and said—

Mr. GRAHAM, prosecution. You need not state what Lasley said.

Q. Now tell what these men did to you?

Mr. GRAHAM: Let us see if they did anything.

The WITNESS: These disguised men you are speaking of?

Q. Yes.

A. They came on me about a week and a half after I moved there. They came to my house and called me out. I heard someone coming—I didn't know what it was. I got up. I had been helping Mr. Thompson kill hogs on that day, and though I was very weary, they came to the door and struck a match and asked me to come out. I told them my wife was a little poorly, I didn't wish to be disturbed to-night, and they said that mattered not, they weren't going to hurt me, to come out.

I opened the door and they said, "Come out." One of them said, "D--n you, if you don't come out I will shoot you."

I walked out then, and there was a small one run up to me and caught me by the back of the neck and said, "D--n you, I've got you now"; and then one said, "You had better hold him or he will run."

I says, "No, sir, I will not run."

Some of them run into the house and said, "Have you got 'ary gun?"

"Yes," said I, "I have got an old gun, but it isn't of much account."

They got hold of it and threw it out of doors, and when they got it out of doors they broke it across a tree. Another of them took my ax out of the house and pitched it off a distance. They then asked me what I thought of them.

I told them I didn't know what to think.

He said, "Damn you, what do you think?"

I said, "I don't know what to think, sir."

He says, "Do you know me?"

I says, "No, I don't know you."

"Well," he says, "D--n you, it is a fine thing you don't." He then says, "Put on our pants."

I put them on.

He said then, "I want you to go toting these things out as soon as you can. Haven't you got any children to help you tote them out?"

I said, "Well, I have got a little boy and two girls"—two daughters, and they were up in the loft asleep—a lying down. I didn't know whether they were asleep or not. One of them caught up a light and ran up there and stamped on the floor and scared them a great deal, and one of them fell down and rolled down the steps. He ran on down after them, and they holloaed to them to tote them things out as fast as they could. They all set in, and my wife set in too and helped carry the things. She had a little baby about three months old. I had killed my hogs and had three of them lying on the floor.

They told me to put everything out. I put my hogs out and then put out the beds and other things; and they went up said, "You have got corn like a white man." They said, "You may put out everything else but your corn and wheat, and you can let them stay till morning, and you must get that out to-morrow." They made me go out then and take some of the fire out of doors and build it up. They said, "If you put anything else back in there I will put you inside, shut the door and burn the house and you in it,"—and, "We have put these things out here and you must stay here till morning." I had hauled a couple of loads of wood the day before, and I made a good fire and they stood over me till I got a fire built.

They began to whisper and talk a little. One of them said to me, "Pull off your shirt." I pulled my shirt off and they said, "Step up there beside that tree and hug the tree." I put my arms around the tree, and one of them said, "D--n you, don't you take your arms away," and they struck me between twenty and thirty licks as nigh as I could give a guess, but they didn't hit me higher than thirty. It hurt pretty bad, I know. When they got done they told me to turn around to the light. I turned around, and he said, "He has got a pretty good whipping." Then he says, "Put on your clothes, boy, and you stay here till day; and if you say anything about this I will come back and kill you."

Q. Where was your family at that time?

A. Standing out there by me.

Q. State who constituted your family at that time.

A. There were eight children and my wife.

Q. Where were they when they were whipping you?

A. They were in the house at that time—two of the children were in the house and my wife, I believe, was in the house and the balance of the children were standing around the fire. I think two of them were in the house.

Q. State whether you were injured by this whipping.

A. Well, I was sore about two weeks, so sore that I could not lie on my back.

Q. Did you do anything for your back?

A. No, sir, only my wife picked out two pieces of stick out of my back. I reckon one of them was about an inch and a half long, and the other was about half an inch.

Q. What kind of instruments did they use in whipping you?

A. Well, I could not give an account—they took it off with them; the pieces that were in my back were hickory.

...

JAMES C. RINGSTAFF *white, 36*

Q. Go on and state your connection with the Kuklux—what you know about it without my asking questions.

A. On the ninth of October, 1869, there were eight or nine men came to my house about eleven o'clock in the night. After halloaing at the door a time they pushed it open and came in and told me that they had understood I had been going to Gappins'—they asked me my name first. When I told them my name they told me that I was the man they were looking for, and that they had understood I had been going to Gappins', and they came around to tell me that if they heard of my being there any more they were going to take me out and hang me to a tree or limb, I am not positive which.

Q. Was there any other time they visited?

A. About the 22nd of December the same year there was some persons came there at night and opened the door and carried out some few things and left notice there. It was written on a piece of paper and also on the door—that if I didn't leave the county in twenty days I "would pass as if from life to death. " They carried out some bed clothing and a chest.

Q. Did they make any other visit?

A. About the 8th of January, 1870, some persons were there again, and at night, I suppose. I was not there all day and went home the next morning, and the visit had been paid—they carried out some things also that night. There were several things that had been carried out from the time I left there until I went back, and also some writing stating that if that house was not cleared of all persons in three days one log would not be on another.

Q. State whether you remained?

A. I did not. I left the second or third day after that, and was gone about two months-and-a-half, I think.

•••

JACOB MURRAY *colored, 50*

Q. Go on and state whether you ever had anything to do with disguised people and tell all about it.

A. Well , sir, I can tell you what they had done when they came to my house. I am a man that wishes to tell the truth. They came to my house, and it was a little gathering—my boy had neighbors come in. I was in there sitting, and I told the boys to ask leave from the boss of the house to pass a little time genteelly. We didn't know anything of the sort was out. They come to the door and they come abreast, I don't know how many. They knocked the door clear off the hinges, and they come and they commenced shooting as quick as they entered in, with little pistols of some sort—went to shooting up above their head, like; and from that they raised an alarm undoubtedly amongst us and frightened us a good deal, and commenced shooting and frightening, unexpected to us all. In the scuffle my little grandchild come to get injured by some means, in this 'ere scuffle that had taken place. That is the way it come to be injured.

They said, after they came to be silent, that they were after Damon [Holt]. They didn't interfere with me any more than that they hurt my feelings on account of my child—that was all. And when they got him settled so that they could get hold of Damon and take him out—

Q. But what about the mother and your grandchild?

A. Well, she had the child in her arms, you know, like a woman will have a child, and they were running, and they seemed in a scuffle. He was scared and they knocked the child out of her arms, and it got mashed somehow or other, underneath. After that, its mother could never raise it up, sir, with no kind of peace, excepting it screamed. She couldn't catch hold of it in no place, to raise it up that it had any pleasure at all. That is the truth.

Q. State how long the child lived.

A. It just lived about two weeks.

Q. State what its condition was before.

A. Well, it was very healthy before this thing had taken place—very healthy apparently, and it was buried over there. I am working at the very place where the child was buried.

Q. Go on and tell what they did after that.

A. Well, after they got them [Damon Holt, Jerry Lynch and Green Freeman] they seemed to get what they called for and seemed to be satisfied; and I told them to let them be quietly, and let the men see what they were going to do; and they got them three out. It seemed like that was their choice. They told me to shut the door and keep the door shut until sunup; and I being the head of the house, I done so—commanded them all to sit in there till that time, and so they did. We didn't go any further with it. I told them all to be quietly till everything got over. It didn't take much of a door to hold them after that. They didn't pretend against opening the door, neither.

Q. Were any of the parties indicted?

A. No, sir.

Q. Why?

A. Well, it is a thing we didn't know how to take hold of to carry out; and if a man takes hold of a thing that he don't understand, he had better let it alone. We come to that conclusion.

JACOB MURRAY, JR.

Q. Go on and state all you know about persons coming to your house—whether they were disguised or not, and all they did.

A. They came there and the door was shut. They broke down the door and threw it in the middle of the floor, and they commenced shooting—I don't how many times they shot.

Q. Who went in there?

A. Well, sir, I didn't know any of them.

Q. State how many, and whether they were disguised.

A. There were eight came in the house, but out of doors I don't know how many there were.

Q. What kind of clothes did they have on?

A. White clothes, and horns. They had long white gowns on.

Q. How were their faces? Did you see their faces?

A. Yes, sir, they had white faces with quills in their mouths—I reckon they were quills, they looked like quills. They were not natural teeth.

Q. Go on and state what they did.

A. Eight of them came in there, and my wife had a baby about four months old, and they run over her, and knocked the child out of my wife's hands and my wife says, "You mustn't kill my child," and she picked it up and the breath was out of the child.

Q. You say they ran over it?

A. Yes, sir, they ran over it, because I saw that myself. She picked it up and shook it a while, and the breath came again after a while, and the child didn't live but a week after they left. It was mashed inside and it never could be better any more. It just lay from that till it died.

Q. State whether it was well before they came there.

A. Yes, sir, it was well and hearty before that night.

Q. How long did you say it lived after that time?

A. It lived a week—just lay and cried just a week after that, and never did get over it till it died.

Q. The men were not there to do anything to you and your wife.

A. Well, sir, they didn't do anything to me; they only just mashed the child; that is all they done.

Q. How did they mash it?

A. Well, they ran over it.

Q. Did they put their feet on it?

A. Yes, sir, they put their feet on it after they knocked it out of her arms.

Q. Just went and put their feet on it?

A. Yes, sir.

Q. You saw them do that?

A. Yes, sir.

Q Didn't you see them go up and kick it?

A. No, sir; they didn't kick it.

Q. Did they stamp it?

A. No, sir; they just went up to it and—

Q. Put their feet on lightly?

A. Yes, sir, just mashed. I don't know whether they put it on lightly or not, they put it on hard enough to mash it.

Q. Just went up to it and put their feet on it?

A. Yes, sir.

Q. Did they stand upon it?

A. They put one foot on it and not their whole weight, I don't reckon.

Q. Did I understand you to say they shot in your house?

A. Yes, sir, they shot. I saw where they shot up against the joist of the house—there was one sprint of a bullet in the log.

Q. They shot up?

A. They shot up in the log. There was a sprint of a bullet in the log; that is all I could see.

Q. How many people were at your home that night?

A. I reckon there were about twenty.

Q. At the dance?

A. Yes, sir.

Q. I understood you to say that this crowd said they didn't want you, they wanted Damon.

A. Yes, sir, they were after Damon they said.

Q. I understood you to say that they ran over the child.

Mr. MERRIMON, prosecution. He didn't say that.

Q. What was it you said about their running over the child and mashing it?

A. I said that my wife was standing in the floor, and they knocked the child out of her—

Q. State how they knocked it out.

A. When they were after Damon, they knocked the child out of her arms.

Q. As they were after Damon—pursuing him?

A. Yes, sir, and then they stepped on the child.

Q. You don't pretend to know whether they did it on purpose or not?

A. No, sir, I can't say whether they did.

Mr. GRAHAM, prosecution. The gentleman is leading the witness all the way.

Mr. MERRIMON, prosecution. He said at first that they knocked the child out of her lap.

Mr. McCORKLE, defense. He said at first that they ran over it.

Q. You say now you don't know whether they did it intentionally or not, but that they were after Damon at that time?

A. Yes. sir.

Mr. BRAGG, prosecution. The objection is that the question is leading.

The CHIEF JUSTICE. I think every senator knows that the witness says they were after Damon and knocked the child out of the woman's arms; and that he does not pretend they did it on purpose.

Mr. BRAGG. The witness stated distinctly on cross-examination, in response to a question, that he saw one of them go up and put a foot on the child.

Mr. McCORKLE, defense. But he did not say the man did it intentionally, and it was with that view that I asked him the question.

Q. How did they carry Green Freeman out?
A. They led him by the hand.

Q. And Lynch also?
A. Yes, sir, led them all out, down in the woods I reckon, about a hundred yards from the house.

Q. Did you hear anything that occurred down there?

A. Yes, sir, I heard them halloaing, and I heard the licks over there in the woods; it was not far from the house—I reckon about a hundred yards. I heard the licks clean from the house. I heard them halloaing, and I heard the licks.

GREEN FREEMAN *colored, 21*

Q. Go on and state what you know about persons going about disguised.

A. I was at this spree at Jake Murray's and the Kuklux came and broke the door down and they called for Damon and hunted around and got him and they took me and Damon and Jerry Lynch out and whipped us. Three of them took me out in the woods and told me to take off my shirt and coat and jacket.

Q. How many licks did they give you?

A. They hit me about six licks apiece; they used pronged switches.

Q. How do you know it was a pronged switch?

A. I saw them when they broke off a limb of a dogwood.

Q. State whether you were badly hurt.

A. Yes, sir, my back was very dreadful the next morning, scars all over my back and welts, there was licks on the back which looked as if there was about seventy-five.

Q. State whether the scars are permanent.

A. Yes, sir, there are some on me now.

Q. Where did you go that night?

A. I went home and got some clothes, then I went out in the woods.

Q. How many rooms were there in that house?

A. One room.

Q. State whether the room was nearly full that evening.

A. It looked nearly full before they came, and when they came it was all filled up in such a pile I could hardly tell, there was a right smart lot

Mr. MERRIMON. Do you pass for a colored or white man?

A. Colored.

Q. Did they state that night what they whipped you for?

A. No, sir.

Q. Do you know what they whipped you for?

A. No, sir.

Q. Why did they take you three out and not take the balance?

A. I don't know.

Q. How big was that house?

A. I don't know how large it was.

Q. How large a room?

A. There was only one room in it; was about as far as here to that post but not quite so large the other way.

Q. About twenty square feet?

A. About twenty feet one way.

The counsel called the name of Jerry Lynch, but there was no response.

Q. Do you know where Jerry Lynch is?

A. He is not here. I have not seen him since that night.

DAMON HOLT *colored, 18*

Q. State whether you have ever seen persons disguised, and all about it.

A. I was at Jacob Murray's house at a frolic and we were in there frolicking and playing and going on, and there were a parcel of disguised people—at least they looked like people—came to the door and bursted the door down and called out for Damon Holt. I was scared and run under the bed, and they come. They called me and I wouldn't answer. They said, "Come out of there; if you don't come out of there, G-d d--n you, I'll shoot you." I got up and came on out, and they gathered me, one by the arm and one by the hand, and told me to follow them, G-d d--n me, that they were going to hang me.

I asked them what they were going go hang me for—I hadn't done anything.

They said, "Never mind, G-d d--n you, I will let you know what I am going to hang you for." They took me then, and one says, "Trot up; if you don't trot up, G-d d--n you, I'll kill you right away." They took a stick and punched me in the back and made me follow them out in the woods about a hundred yards from Jacob Murray's house, and there they took my shirt off and made me hug around a tree, and gave me about sixty licks, I reckon. I was so scared I didn't count the licks, but from the marks on my back it looked like they gave me about sixty or seventy licks—some three or four of them. Four whipped me at a time; and then they turned me loose and told me to run.

I then took a run down into the hollow back towards the house, and they shot at me. I ran on up towards the fence, got to the fence and went into the barn and lay there all night.

Q. Whose barn did you go into?

A. Mr. Joseph Merritt's.

Q. You lay there all night?

A. Yes, sir, lay there till day break and then came back and got my clothes.

Q. State whether it was warm weather or not.

A. No, sir, it was pretty cool weather.

Q. You had no clothes?

A. No clothes on, sir, at all; I didn't have any clothes, any more than my pants; had my pants on, but had no shirt on at all. They tore my shirt all to pieces—off of me.

Q. How many of them whipped you?

A. There were four whipped me at once.

Q. How did the four manage to whip you at once?

A. They made me kneel down, and they just whipped me all over my head and all over me every-which-way—all around.

Q. Whilst you were hugging the tree?

A. Yes, sir, I was hugging the tree—down on my knees hugging the tree; and they shot me—they didn't shoot me with a gun, but with a hickory, all over my head back here, and the scars are on me now.

Q. You say they shot at you?

A. Yes, sir, they shot at me after I left.

Q. When you were running?

A. Yes, sir, they told me to run; when they got done whipping me they said, "G-d d--n you, now run." I got up then and ran, and they shot at me as I was running.

Q. How far were you from them when they shot at you?

A. I was about as far from them as from here to that side of the house [*indicating the end of the senate chamber, about fifteen steps*].

Q. State if any other persons were carried out at the same time that you were.

A. Yes, sir, Green Freeman and Jerry Lynch were carried out at the same time. They whipped them. They whipped us sort of in a line; the furthest one was as far from me as from me to you, and the next one about as far as half way betwixt me and you. They whipped me last. Green Freeman ran around through the woods there. I don't know what became of him. He went on home, I guess, for I never saw him anymore that night. And then they whipped Jerry, and Jerry went on over the fence apiece, and he was lying down in the corner of the fence, and I came upon him, and he and I got together there and went on to Mr. Merritt's barn and lay there.

Q. State what they said they whipped you for.

A. They never said what they whipped me for.

Q. Describe the noise that these people made.

A. Well, they made a fuss like a cat and like chickens, a fuss like dogs.

Q. Why didn't you indict them?

A. I was scared and afraid if I done anything or said anything they might come and kill me.

...

SIMON WHITE *colored*

Q. How old are you?
A. I don't know.

Q. Where do you live?
A. I live in Chatham.

Prosecution. We object to the testimony unless the act were shown to have come from Alamance County.

Mr. McCORKLE, defense. We will show that the outrage were committed by Alamance men.

A. Some men came to my house and whipped me. They took me out in the yard and whipped me. Two took hold of me, one on each side, and held me out and they whipped me about twenty licks, I believe.

Q. What did they whip you with?
A. Some of them had a plaited switch, some persimmon and some dogwood.

Q. How did they hold you?
A. They held me in this way [*the witness held out his arms horizontally*]. They had each arm stretched out in that way.

Q. Where were you living?
A. At William Stout's.

Q. State the nature of the whipping you got.
A. I was very sore.

Q. How long?
A. For two or three days.

Mr. MERRIMON, prosecution. What did they whip you for?
A. I cannot tell exactly what.

Q. Tell as near as you can.

A. They said they whipped me because I eat with white folks. Some said so, and some said they whipped me to make an equality with the white folks.

Q. Didn't they charge you with stealing?

A. No, sir.

Q. Were you ever charged with stealing?

A. No, sir.

Q. Were you ever whipped before?

A. No, sir.

Q. Were you a slave or a free man?

A. I was always a free man.

Q. Born free?

A. Yes, sir.

William Stout, 59, white, testified that White had been allowed to eat at his table occasionally, that he slept in the kitchen in the loft by himself, but not in the same house.

Q. Has he ever slept in the big house?

A. Not that I know of.

Q. Do you belong to the Society of Friends?

A. Yes, sir.

...

MARY GAPPINS *white, 46*

Q. Go on and state if anything was done to you by disguised persons, and if so, when it was.

A. My house was torn down from over my head on the 8th of last January was twelve months ago.

Q. Where did you live?

A. About ten miles from Graham courthouse down south.

Q. How many were in your family?

A. Six. My children and myself.

Q. How old are they?

A. One was a married daughter twenty-three years old, she was living with me; another was twenty years old and the other two are small, one nine and the other five, and then my daughter's child is about three years old.

Q. What condition did they come in?

A. They came in white pants and robing with belts fastened around like. They had no gowns on but they had something over their head, which did not quite cover all of their head for I saw their natural hair. Then they had marks, little red marks on the faces of them and they had something like horses' mane which hung down for a beard—at least they lost one of them and I saw it. They didn't have it fastened on very well.

Q. Did you get it.

A. Yes, sir.

Q. That was horse hair?

A. Yes, sir, it was a mane or horse hair of some kind, whatever you may call it. It belonged to horses anyhow.

Q. Were you abed?

A. Me and my two oldest daughters were sitting by the fire. The children were in bed. It was cold weather, the coldest night there had been that winter,—at least the neighbors said it was. I did not get cold that night, for I was too mad to be cold.

Q. Did you get mad?

A. I did, for it was enough to make anybody mad.

Q. Tell us how they commenced their operations.

A. They came to the door; my dog barked and Caroline spoke up and said here is some one. I said, "Who is it?"

She said Julia said, "The Klux is coming" and she counted and said there were seven of them in the yard. They came close to the door and spoke. Then one of the girls, I don't know which, said, "come in" or "scratch under"—I don't know which. They come in and said we had to get out in fifteen minutes, or else the house would be torn down. The girls went to the door and asked them what they were going to tear the house down for. I was sitting by the fire. I would not go to the door and I did not say a word to them. They said they had orders to tear down the house. I still did not go to the door.

Q. Who did they say gave the order?

A. They said that they had got the order from headquarters. The girls kept asking them about it and told them not to tear the house down, but they said they would, and told them to take the things out, and they turned in and took the things out and put them in the yard, and after that, they tore down the house and started off. As they started off, I said I think this is a pretty trick for my neighbors' boys. They got up in a club together and whispered, I reckon, I don' t know what they said, but they stepped back and said, "If you are not

out of the county in a few days, or come back, you are dead."
I made no answer, but I have not left the county yet.

Q. They tore your house down?

A. Yes, sir, they tore it down to the bottom log.

Q. And took your things out?

A. Yes, sir, they did not damage them much.

Q. Did you know any of them?

A. I know the last one of them. I knew them when they
were not more than knee high to a man. [*As she is naming the
men, the trial transcript notes parenthetically, "Persons in the
court here exhibited some merriment."*] You may laugh if you
want to, but I have come here to speak the truth and I will if
I am killed the next minute for it.

Q. What is your occupation?

A. My occupation is to work for a living and stay at home
and mind my own business.

Q. What sort of work do you do?

A. Any that I can.

Q. Have you ever been married?

A. No, sir. I have not.

Q. How many children have you?

A. I have had seven.

Q. How many colored children?

A. I never had but one, I thank you. [*laughter*]

Q. Are persons in the habit of visiting your house—men?

A. No, sir.

Q. White men come there occasionally.

A. They come sometimes of course.

Q. Do colored men come there?

A. No, sir, they do not come for any such business. [*laughter*]

Q. How did you come to have that colored child?

A. It was a darkey who took me in some way and got me where I could not help myself. [*laughter*] I have as much objection to white folks and darkies mixing up as anybody. [*laughter*]

Q. I ask you if you don't keep a common brothel?

A. No, sir, I do not; that cannot be made to appear against me with truth.

Q. You are not a lewd woman?

A. I never was; if I am accused of it, I am accused of it falsely. What I did I did myself and made no fuss about it to anybody. [*laughter*]

JULIA GAPPINS *white, also testified about this event.*

Q. Go on and tell all that took place up your way.

A. On Saturday night some people came there and tore our house down.

Q. When?

A. Over twelve months ago. I do not remember what month it was now. They did not tell me what they tore it down for. I asked them what they did it for and they said it was orders from headquarters from Petersburg.

Q. Tell what was said when they came.

A. I cannot tell what they said. They came to the door, and put through their heads, and I told them to "Come in" or "scratch under." They didn't come in, and I opened the door and they told us to get out of the house, as they were going to tear it down in fifteen minutes. I asked them what they were going to tear down the house for, but they would not make any answer. They told us to take the things out. I told them if they wanted to have the things out quicker than I could get them out they had better take hold and help. The four came in, and I asked them if they had got anything against me, and they said they would not hurt a hair on my head.

Q. Did they tear it down?

A. Yes, sir, they tore it down to the ground.

Q. What kind of weather was it?

A. The coldest night there was in the year—that is what the neighbors said.

Q. What did you do after they tore the house down?

A. We stayed out of doors.

Q. What sort of a night was it?

A. It was a clear night—it was moonshine.

Q. Where did you go the next morning—what did you do?

A. We just stayed out of doors. We didn't go anywhere. We fixed up a tent out of doors.

Q. How long did you live in the tent?

A. Thirteen months and twenty days I believe.

Q. What did they do after the house was torn down?

A. After they tore the house down they talked a few words and Mother said, "It is a nice trick for my neighbours' boys," and they said if we didn't go out of the county in ten days they would come back and we would be dead.

...

DONALDSON WORTH *colored*

Q. Where do you reside?

A. Cane Creek.

Q. What county?

A. Alamance—the dividing line between Alamance and Chatham—right on the line.

Q. How far from the Moore County line?

A. Oh, sir, the Moore County line is some thirty miles.

Q. How far from the Orange County line?

A. The Orange County line is some twenty-five miles, I guess.

Q. State whether you ever saw any disguised persons in Alamance County, when it was and where it was, and all about it, and what they did to you.

A. No, sir, not in Alamance County. I saw them in Chatham County.

Manager SPARROW, prosecution. Never mind about Chatham. Where did the parties come from?

A. They came out of Alamance County.

Mr. MERRIMON, prosecution. The senate has ruled that it will not hear anything about these transactions outside of Alamance and Caswell counties.

Q. How far from the county line did you see these men?

A. About a quarter of a mile, sir.

Q. Do you know which direction they were coming from?

A. They were coming from towards Alamance County—out from the line, from towards Alamance County.

Mr. MERRIMON. How do you know they came from towards Alamance?

A. I told you I did not know; it was supposed that they came from that way, because they came from that course. That is the reason why.

Q. Could you tell from their voices who they were?

A. Well, I was too nigh scared to death to tell much of anything.

Q. How long were you with them?

A. They had me out some hour and a half, I reckon.

Q. Did you hear them talk much?

A. Yes, sir, they talked, but they talked point blank like a parcel of geese. It is hard understanding what a parcel of geese say.

Q. What did they do?

A. They bursted the door open and took me out of bed and ordered me to rise; I jumped up; they caught hold of me and slipped a rope around my neck and told me they were going to take me out to hang me; I begged of him, "Please gentlemen do not hang me." I said I was not fitted to die.

They ordered me to shut my mouth and struck me on the side of the head with a cane and carried me down to a big poplar tree and told me to get down on my knees and pray. I was then scared to death and begged them not to hang me. He says, "You must not call us gentlemen at all."

I said, "I will call you just what you say I must call you."

He said, "You must call us Mr. Kuklux, that is our name—that is the name you should call us."

I said, "I will call you any name you wish me to."

Then they quarreled as to what they should do, whether they should hang me or whip me and decided they would whip me and not hang me. They took me down to a poplar tree and pulled me with a rope. I thought they were going to hang me, I had no doubt about it. They tied the rope a little tight so that I could not holloa and they struck me twenty-five licks—five men struck me five licks a piece with a leather strap and then turned me loose, or untied me from the tree and led me up on the hill.

They carried me in a field and made me get on my knees, and put a sword against my breast and gave me the law and told me what the law was—their law, that whenever I met a white person, no matter who he was, whether he was poor or rich, I was to take off my hat and put it under my arm.

I told them that I had always done that.

The next thing was that if I met a lady passing, I had to walk on the opposite side of the road and not to walk so as to meet her.

I told him that I would try to do it, that I would follow the law that they had laid down for us to follow.

They then turned me loose and I went on to my house; they told me that they whipped me because they had been informed that I had arms to kill the Kuklux with.

I told them that it was only a mistake, that I had none; that I had never owned a gun—only an old holster pistol.

They said they understood I had got Bowie knives. They went and got the pistol while they had me in the wood. I told them that I had not got any Bowie knives; I told them that I had some knives that my master in his life time let me have. I used to keep his knives and spaying needles and he gave them to me. They took them and carried them off with the pistol. They told me that I must obey this law, because it was their constitution, and I told them that I would do it.

Q. What did they say they whipped you for?

A. They said I had been saucy to white people, and I had accumulated arms to kill the Kuklux.

...

ALFRED WHITE *colored, 53*

Q. Go on and tell what was done to you.

A. There were five disguised men come to my house and took me out of my house and whipped me. Three of them struck me three licks apiece with a wagon whip with a leather strap attached to the end of it. They did not hurt me much only where it struck one of my fingers.

Q. How did they get in the house?

A. They came to the door. They run against it, all hands, and said, "D--n you, open the door." I was lying on the bed and got up and put on my pants, but before I got them on they run against it several times, and finally they got a rail to burst the door open, but I went to the door and opened it, and as soon as I did they gathered me in by the arms. They did not come in, but just as I opened it wide enough the men gathered me by the hands and pulled me out.

I stepped off about fifteen or twenty steps. At this time there commenced a right smart racket in the house. There was one on each side of me and two had gone into the house and gathered a chair. The dog had commenced barking at them and they took that chair and beat it on the floor and broke it to pieces to pester the dog who was under the bed. Then one of these said come back and they came out and stopped the fuss and we all went about a hundred yards from the house.

Q. Who was in the house?

A. My wife and children. Then one of my daughters who had been married and her husband were there.

Q. They gave you nine lashes only, but they didn't hurt you much?

A. Only one.

Q. Where was that?

A. That was on my finger. I had my finger down and I think there was a knot on the lash and that hit my finger.

Q. What did they whip you with?

A. A wagon whip and it had a leather at the end of the lash and a knot on the end.

Q. What did they whip you for?

A. I don't know. They first said that I had been talking saucy to white men. I told them that that was a mistake; that was a thing I had never done and I could prove to the contrary, and I said that that was not so.

Then they said, "You are guilty of white women."

I said, "That is not so," that they might have heard it but it was not so.

Q. They charged you with keeping a white woman?

A. Yes, sir.

Q. And charged you with insolence to white people?

A. Yes, sir.

Q. I ask you if you didn't keep several white women?

A. No, sir.

Q. Are you a miller?

A. Yes, sir, and that is the reason why they charged me; because people of all kinds and colors came to the mill, women and men. No person could say it in my settlement. I was born and raised in Alamance County.

Q. Were you born free or were you born a slave?

A. I was born free.

Q. And you say you were not saucy to white people?

A. No, sir, I was not.

...

JOHN OVERMAN *colored, 23*

Q. Go on and state whether you have ever seen any person disguised, and all you know about it.

A. They came to my house and burst my door open and come in and took me out of bed and cut off one side of my beard and one side of my hair. They took me out in the yard and ten of them struck me two licks a piece.

Q. How far did they carry you from the house?

A. Only in the yard.

Q. They broke your door down?

A. They did not break it down, they bursted it open; they bursted the latch off.

Q. The ten came in?

A. Yes, sir.

Q. Do you know any of them?

A. I know one.

Q. What was his name?

A. Cicero McPherson.

Q. How did you know him?

A. I knew him by his voice. I was very well acquainted with him.

Q. What did Cicero McPherson want to whip you for?

A. Because of my pitching around a woman.

Q. I thought you were married.

A. I was.

Q. But you "pitch" around anyhow?

A. Yes, sir, like ever one else does. [*laughter*]

Q. They charged you with what—had you ravished a woman?
A. No, sir.

Q. Did they charge you with keeping a woman?
A. Yes, sir.

Q. She was not your wife?
A. Yes, sir.

Q. You were guilty of that, were you not?
A. Of course I was. [*laughter*]

Q. Had you treated your wife badly at all?
A. No, sir, I had not treated her badly.

Q. Why didn't you indict them?
A. Because I did not think it was worthwhile. They were pretty thick around there and if I undertook to do anything I thought they would come again.

Q. "They were pretty thick about there"—what do you mean by that?
A. These disguised men.

Q. You were afraid on that account?
A. Yes, sir.

Mr. Sparrow, prosecution. Don't you think you deserved all you got?
A. Yes, sir. [*laughter*]

...

GREEN LANKFORD *colored, 71*

Q. What is your age?

A. If I live till the middle of June, I will be 72.

Q. Where do you reside?

A. At Jim Holt's factory.

Q. Will you state what you know about seeing disguised persons—when it was and all about it?

A. Yes, sir, I can tell you what I know about it. There were seven come to my house and dragged me and my wife out of bed one night and took me out into the woods in my night clothes and stripped my clothes off and struck me fifteen licks.

Q. State how they got you out of the house.

A. Why, they broke the lock, sir.

Q. What time was this?

A. I reckon it has been about twelve months as well as I can recollect.

Q. You say you were taken out of your bed by these men?

A. Yes, sir, I was certainly. It was about one o'clock, as near as I could get at it.

Q. How far did they carry you from the house?

A. As nigh as I could guess, about three hundred yards, I reckon.

Q. Did I understand you to say they carried Mrs. Lankford also?

A. They dragged her out of the bed, but they never carried her.

Q. Did they offer any other indignities to her except that?

A. No, sir, not that I know of.

Q. Will you state whether you were injured?

A. Well, you can judge as you please, gentlemen—I was hit fifteen licks on the naked skin.

Q. We cannot well judge ourselves.

A. Well, I cannot tell any more. You know how whipping hurts, I reckon? [*laughter*]

Q. You can state whether it was painful or not?

A. Of course it was.

Q. How long did it remain so?

A. Some four, five or six days.

Q. What did they whip you for?

A. Well, that you will have to find out, my friend.

Q. Didn't they tell you?

A. They said my wife had it done, but I don't know whether that was so or not.

Q. How did you and your wife live together?

A. Well, as good as anybody in the world.

Q. Were you peaceable?

A. Yes.

Q. Quiet?

A. Yes, sir, never had a bit of fuss in our lives.

Q. Never in the world?

A. No, sir.

Q. Didn't you load your gun and tell your wife you were going to shoot her?

A. No, sir.

Q. I will put you on your guard.

A. I don't care if you do. You cannot scare me—I ain't to be scared by such.

Q. But you are liable to the law if you don't tell the truth.

A. I am telling the truth.

Q. You didn't have any dispute with your wife?

A. No, sir. I have had two wives, and I am just as clear as you are. [*laughter*]

Q. What I do is not the question. Have you from time to time had quarrels with your wife?

A. No, sir.

Q. Didn't you load your gun and threaten to shoot her?

A. Maybe you was one of them. [*laughter*]

Q. I ask you if you did not load your gun and threaten to shoot your wife?

A. No, I did not.

The CHIEF JUSTICE. You can name some particular time that you suppose or allege he handled a gun, or threatened his wife.

The WITNESS. I want him to tell how he got up about the gun business. [*laughter*]

Q. It is none of your business how we got it.

A. My friend, you might get hurt yourself maybe.

Q. When you get into a controversy with your wife you are not as offensive towards her as you are towards me, are you—you don't get out of humor?

A. No, sir, she don't ask me such lies.

Q. I do not understand what you said they whipped you for.

A. They said my wife had it done.

Q. Well, what for?

A. They didn't say for what—I don't know for what.

. . .

MARY HOLT *colored*

Q. What is your husband's name?

A. Henry Holt.

Q. Do you recollect the night that Outlaw was hung?

A. Yes, sir. They broke in my house and asked for Henry, and I told them he was not at home. Then they asked me where he was. I told them I didn't know. Some of them allowed I did and I would have to tell. I told them I couldn't tell, for I didn't know where he was. They said if I didn't tell where he was they would shoot me. I told them they would have to shoot, for I couldn't tell them where he was. Some of them said I would have to get up and go with them, and I asked if I could take my baby with me. One of them said no, to lie still, that I needn't go.

Q. What else did they do?

A. They didn't say anything more, but asked if he stayed there all night, and I told them not often, sometimes he did and sometimes he didn't, and they told me when they started out to tell him that if he was not gone from there the next Saturday night, and left Graham he would be gone up. Then they went out and came back again and asked me for a piece of rope. I told them there wasn't none there only what was in the bed, and they asked me which bed the cord was in. I told them it was in the bed I was lying in, and they told me to get up then, they would have to have a piece of it; so I got out of bed and they cut a piece out of the bed-cord.

Q. How long a piece?

A. They cut from the head end to the foot. It was a hemp cord, about the size of my middle finger, as near as I can guess at it.

Q. Did they take it away?

A. Yes, sir, they took it away.

Q. Do you know anything about Outlaw being hung that night?

A. No, sir, I don't know anything about it.

Q. Did you see him the next morning?

A. No, sir, I have never seen him.

Q. Didn't see the rope?

A. No, sir, I never went out the next morning.

Q. Who broke in?

A. The Kuklux they call them. They were dressed in white and had gowns on.

• • •

JEMIMA PHILIPS *colored, 74*

Q. What is your age?

A. I shall be 75 if I live to see the 20th day of August.

Q. Did you know Wyatt Outlaw?

A. He was my son.

Q. State who came there and when the last time you saw your son.

A. Well, when I woke up out of my sleep, there were about 20 that come into my room.

Q. How did they get into the house?

A. They bursted a piece of the button off the door; they could not get the button off; it was held by a screw and they bursted half the piece where the button was on and came in.

Q. Go on and tell about it.

A. They had great torches lighted. First they came and threw the cover off of me.

Q. Go on now and tell all they did and said.

A. Then they said to me, "Where is Wyatt—where is Henry Holt?" One says, "Say! say! say!" There were two who had swords and there were pistols. One said, "Cut her head off," and another said, "Blow her brains out."

They went out of that room and as they passed, one says to the other, "Let us set the house afire," and they went around to the room and I heard the little child cry—that is the baby—"Oh Daddy! Oh Daddy!" I was at the middle door and I ran and opened that door and they were standing with the light so [*illustrating*] and they were all around him.

Q. Whom are you talking about—about whom?

A. All around my son.

Q. Who was he?

A. Wyatt Outlaw. He was putting on his pants, and I run back and got a stick and laid away as hard as I could. They jumped on me, they did, three of them, and stamped me, and I arose three times and they knocked me down and then I holloaed for murder, and they went off with him.

Q. Went off with whom?

A. With my child out of that room. Just led him off. He had not got his pants on, and they did not let him get his hat or anything but just get his pantaloons on. They went right out towards the blacksmith's shop, and made him climb the fence, and went down the street. It was all bright, as they had torches so that we could see.

Q. When did you see him after that time?

A. I never saw him any more until they sent for me to the court house after they had cut him down. He was lying on the bench—whatever it was, in the court house.

Q. He was alive?

A. No, sir.

Q. He was dead?

A. He was dead. They hung him on the 26th day of the month, the Sunday was the 27th, and he was buried the last day, twelve months ago.

Q. I understood you to say that when they started in that room you attempted to strike some of them? Did you?

A. No, sir, they went out of the door; I never hit them only when I opened the door, and they were standing in the room, as I say; they were surrounding him, and I say who would not fight for their child.

Q. That is what I understood. You say that when they got around him, then you commenced striking?

A. When they got around him he was sitting putting his pants on, and a little baby child of his said, "Oh Daddy! Oh Daddy!" and then I went and opened the door and went in there, and they had him with his pants on and they took him right out of that door.

Q. You don't answer my question; I ask you what you did to them, where you raised that stick?

A. I said I struck at them as hard as I could.

Q. I understand that; now what did they do after you struck them?

A. They stamped me.

Q. Did they say anything to you?

A. Yes, sir, after they stamped me they said, "G-d d--n you, you strike a white man?" and they stamped me three times, in my breast and on my head and arms.

Q. Did they have any arms?

A. Yes, sir, they had arms.

Q. What did they have?

A. They didn't have no gloves nor nothing.

Q. I ask you if they had weapons—not arms like mine or yourself.

A. They had some arms like mine and yours.

Q. He means did they have any guns?

A. They had swords and pistols and a sassafras stick.

...

MATILDA PURYEAR *colored*

Q. Were you at home the night William Puryear was taken off?

A. Yes, sir, I was at home.

Q. Tell all you know about that.

A. I was there when the company came in there, betwixt midnight and day, and took him out. They just pushed open the door and came in. I was asleep, and they woke me up when they came in. He called me when they came in to come to him, and I started to him. One of them ran up to me and told me "G-d d--n you, stand back," or he would cut my head off; and they took him out of doors and commenced talking to him. They took him out with one shoe on and no hat.

Q. What did they say to him?

A. When they came in they told him to come out. One of them says, "Come and go with me." He took him out into the yard, took him out there a right smart bit, and then come in and asked me for his gun. I told them where it was, and they went and got it. They told me to get up and shut the door, and I got up and went to fasten the door, but they had fastened it outside, and they told me not to open it until the next morning, until sun up.

Q. How did you get out in the morning?

A. My little boy climbed out of the chimney, and undone the door.

Q. When was it you last saw your husband's body?

A. I don't know what month it was when I saw it, but the wheat was turning right smart, when they took him out.

Q. Took him out of what?

A. Out of the water-course.

Q. Where?

A. Haw Creek, Dr. Wilson's mill pond.

Q. Do you know it was your husband?

A. All I went by was the buttons on his clothes, big brass buttons, and he didn't have on but one shoe.

Q. Was the body much decayed?

A. Yes, sir, it was all mortified, powerful. I say it was near about rotted—his body.

Q. You couldn't recognize him by his face?

A. No, sir.

Q. Was there anything tied to your husband's feet when he was taken out of the water?

A. Yes, sir, there was a rock to one of them.

Q. Who found him first?

A. Some of the neighbors found him by the buzzards.

Q. What was the condition of your husband at the time he was taken away?

A. Well, he was near about distracted. He said that evening that he felt uneasy; he was afraid somebody would kill him.

...

ELI OUTLAW *colored*

Q. State your name, age and residence.

A. My name is Eli Outlaw. I do not know my age. I live in Graham.

Q. Go on and state whether you ever saw any persons disguised and if so, when, and where, and all about it.

A. Well, sir, I have never seen them but once, and I didn't have a fair sight at them then. It was in my house on the night that they shot in there. I saw them passing through the crack of the door.

Q. How many?

A. I cannot say—a pretty smart crowd, but I didn't count them.

Q. How far were you from them?

A. I was in my house and they were all around it.

Q. Tell what they did.

A. They shot into my house and kept up a terrible fuss around it, beating and lamming—in fact, they pulled off one of the boards and they shot through that place.

Q. One of the boards from where?

A. Off the backside of the house. I found three holes that came through. The others lodged and didn't get through. One of the balls I picked up out of the floor the next morning.

Q. How many did you have in your family?

A. My wife and two children at that time.

Q. State whether their position in the house at the time of the shooting in was such that they were endangered by it, or not.

A. Well, they were in bed when the shooting was done, and the balls did not go across the bed. After the shooting ceased, I got up and left the house—after they left there.

Q. Where did you go to?

A. I went over in the field a short distance from the house, and there I lay all night—the balance of the night.

Q. Who went with you?

A. My wife and children.

Q. State what you carried with you to keep comfortable.

A. I carried only two quilts.

Q. How far did you go from the house?

A. I suppose one hundred and fifty yards.

Q. State whether it was in a field, or in woods, or where.

A. In a field.

Q. How long do you say you staid there?

A. Well, I staid from the time they came until day. I suppose it was—well, it was early in the night when they aroused me, and they did not come around the house only a short time till they left, and when they left I left.

Q. Did you hear any remarks they made at the time they were around your house? Anything they said?

A. No, sir, only the one word when they first came up and commenced beating and knocking around. They said, "Rally out, G-d d--n you, rally out!"—just so.

Q. Whom were they talking to?

A. I don't know that.

Q. You did "rally out" at the back door afterwards?

A. I "rallied out" after they left.

Q. Where were you the night of Wyatt Outlaw's hanging?

A. I was in the mountain working on the public railroad.

Q. How old are you?

A. I don't know.

Q. Don't know whether you are old enough to vote or not?

A. I have voted.

Q. What side did you vote on?

A. The republican side.

...

GEORGE D. BOONE *white, 52*

Q. Do you hold any office?

A. Yes, sir, I am postmaster at Company's Shops.

Q. Did you ever get any warning about your safety?

A. Yes, sir, last month a year ago.

Q. What was it?

A. It was posted up on a tree on the road from the railroad office where I passed through to my office. I went and took the paper down from the tree. The first thing on the paper was a tree. It was drawn on the paper with myself and two colored men, Alfred Trollinger and Levi Barton. Then there were three coffins on the picture, and on each one of the coffins was one of our names.

Q. What was the inscription?

A. Along on the corner was written, "You three d----d sons of b-----s, we intend to get shut of you." Then below that was my name with, "You d----d son of a b----h, we intend to coil this rope around your neck."

Q. Anybody's name signed to it?

A. Three K's.

...

SALLY HOLT *white*

Q. Did you see any disguised men?

A. Yes, sir.

Q. Did they come inside your house?

A. Yes, sir, they came inside.

Q. State what they said and did to you.

A. Well, there were a couple of boys there, and they took them out. I cannot tell what they did with them.

Q. What did they say they were going to do?

A. They didn't say what they were going to do. They told them to come out.

Mr. GRAHAM, prosecution. I would like to have the witness describe this scene without interrogation.

Mr. SMITH, defense. I wish she would.

The WITNESS. They never came back to the house after they took these boys out.

Q. They were carried off, and never came back to your house?

A. Yes, sir, they came back once more.

Q. No, I mean those boys?

A. Yes, sir, the boys were there after that. They came back that night and got their coats after they left.

Q. They went off then without their coats?

A. Yes, sir. They took them off without their coats on.

Q. Do you know whether they had been whipped?

A. They said they hadn't.

Q. Did you see any marks about their persons?

A. No, sir.

Mr. GRAHAM. It is not evidence. She said they said they had not been whipped.

Q. What boys were they—what were their names?

A. Alson Shoe and Lewis Baines.

Q. Was there any other time when disguised men came to your house?

A. Yes, one time after that. They came there one night—we were all gone to bed—and halloaed. I got up, but before I could get up they opened the door and came in and accused me of telling they had been there. They said they had heard I told that the Kuklux were there. They said if I ever told again they would kill me.

Q. Was this second visit they paid you before they took your door down?

A. Yes, sir.

Q. Did they come to your house at any other time?

A. Yes, sir, they came there once. I was not at home, and they threw my things out.

Q. Just state what you found when you got home.

A. I found the things sitting out in the yard.

Q. Was anything broken?

A. No, sir, only the door was torn down.

Q. What did they pull your house down for?

A. They did not pull it down.

Q. What did they take your things out for?

A. I could not tell you, I was not at home; I was off to work the day before.

Q. What were these young men doing in your house that night?

A. Well, I don't know. They said they came to see my boy. There was one young man, he had just come in from Indiana.

Q. Did you have any daughters?

A. Yes, sir, I have two.

Q. Did they go to see these girls?

A. They did not say they did.

Q. Did they go to bed with the girls?

A. No, sir.

Q. What did they have their coats off for?

A. They were sitting before the fire. They had been playing like all young folks.

Q. Didn't they go to bed that night with your daughters?

A. No, sir.

Q. With you?

A. No, sir, we were all up.

Q. Was it complained in the neighborhood that you kept a sort of bad house?

A. No, sir. Some of them had such a chat—

Q. You did not?

A. No, sir, I didn't.

Q. Are you a married woman?

A. I have been married.

Q. Is your husband living now?

A. My husband is dead.

Q. When did he die?

A. He died about the time of the surrender, or a little after.

Q. Have you had any children since his death?

A. No, sir.

Q. Did you keep a nice house?

A. I always tried to do it as nigh as I knew how. I never kept anything else if I knew it.

POLLY HOLT *white, also testified about this event.*

Q. Do you know anything about the house being broken open and the furniture being put out in the yard?

A. Yes, sir, it was. When we went home the next morning—we were not at home that night—the things were lying out in the yard.

Q. Was the furniture put out carefully or not?

A. It was laid out and there was nothing broken.

Q. Did you see the door?

A. Yes, sir.

Q. Was it broken?

A. It was lying in the yard before the door off the hinges.

Q. What did those young men come to your house for the first night?

A. Well, they came there and said they wanted to see my brother. They were going on up to his uncle's. Bane was going to his uncle Bill's.

Q. Didn't they go to bed?

A. No, sir.

Q. Are you sure of that?

A. Yes, sir.

Q. They didn't talk to you that night?

A. Not when they came back.

Q. Before they went away didn't they talk with you?

A. No secret talk.

Q. What were their coats off for?

A. They were playing around there.

Q. What time of the year was it—cold or hot weather?

A. It was so long ago I don't know, I have forgotten.

Q. Had you a fire?

A. Yes, sir, we had on a fire.

Q. A big fire?

A. Yes, sir, a big fire.

Q. It must have been cold weather?

A. Well, they were fooling around with my brother, scuffling and pulling his coat off.

Q. Have you ever been married?

A. No, sir.

Q. Have you got any children?

A. Yes.

Q. White or black?

A. White.

Q. You say when they first went there they had black gowns on?

A. Yes, sir, the first time they came there they were all dressed like—

Q. I notice you spit very much. Do you chew tobacco?

A. Yes, sir.

...

HAMILTON BRIEN *colored, 39*

Q. State what you know about disguised men and if you have ever seen any, and if so, under what circumstances.

A. They came to my house this March twelve months ago.

Q. What did they do to you and tell how many came.

A. Some fifteen came there. They came to the door and knocked at it and told me to open it. I got up and went to the door and three men gathered hold of me and one said, "G-d d--n you, you buss a white woman, will you"? He said, "If you deny it, I will kill you." Then four or five tore off my shirt and held me there, one arm each way. One asked, "Who lives in that house?"

I said, "John Fogleman."

They took me by the arm and led me before his door and they called for John Fogleman and he came and they shook him a little and then turned him loose. They said, "Don't hurt him, he is an officer." I stood there naked some time and they went backwards and forwards in the house. Then they came out and formed a line. They made a ring and set me up in the middle. He says, "Don't hit him any more licks than I do and don't hit him any harder." He struck eight and handed the whip to the balance and they kept on in that way all whipping around me.

After they had done whipped me, they said they wanted to shoot my dog.

I told them to shoot him.

He said, "I will not shoot him, but you may shoot him yourself."

They went into the house and they took everything there was in it. I had a daughter in the house who had a baby two weeks old; she ran out barefooted and wanted Mr. Fogleman to let her in his house but he never let her in. At that time there was a crowding around and they made my women go in.

Q. What women?

A. My women. After then I went back and stayed there a while, they said, "You will have to go in ten days."

I said, "Where am I to go?"

He said, "You are to go in the woods and take fare like I do. If you are not gone in ten days we will come back and hang you."

I said, "Must I go back in my house?"

He said, "You are not going in your house."

I stayed in the yard and they started over the fence and I commenced picking up the things and putting them in the house and I laid [out] there and slept until morning.

Q. What was your condition when they whipped you, was your shirt off?

A. They whipped me with my wagon whip and when they were done they dropped it in the yard. They hurt me right smart and raised some welts but they didn't cut the skin open.

Q. You say that after your daughter went to Folgleman's and wanted to get in they were ordered to return into the house.

A. Yes, sir.

Q. What did they order them to do?

A. They told them to go back into the house—that they were not going to interfere with them.

Q. How old was this child of your daughter's?

A. Two weeks old. My daughter had never been out of the bed until that night since the child was born.

Q. Did all your family run out?

A. Yes, sir.

Q. How far did they go from your house?

A. Not ten steps. I was right in front of John Fogleman's when they whipped me.

Q. You were never whipped in your life?

A. No, sir. I had four masters and never one of them whipped me.

...

LINN B. HOLT *white, 28*

Q. Will you go on and state whether you have ever seen any person disguised, and when it was—all about it.

A. Sometime about the 1st of April, a disguised party of men came to my house—some twelve or fifteen in number—they called at my gate and told me not to be alarmed. I did so and they asked me how things were going on in the neighborhood. I told them, as far as I knew, everybody was behaving themselves, and so on. They told me where they had been, and what they had done. They told me they had been up to see Ham, a negro that lives some two miles from my house; said they didn't think he had been behaving himself as he ought to have done.

Q. What did they say they had done to him?

A. They said they had dressed him off.

Q. Was there any reference in that conversation to the hanging of Outlaw?

A. They said that Outlaw had been hung and told me to tell William Albright—Bill Albright—that there were others to be hung—that they had understood that Albright had organized his party to devastate the county, and to appoint some time and place and they would meet them. Other persons had to be hung.

Q. What time in the night was it?

A. It was between twelve and one o'clock.

...

WILLIAM J. WARD *colored, 53*

Q. Go on and state without my asking any questions how the Kuklux treated you—all about it and when it was—all about it.

A. Well, I suppose about midnight I was waked up by a noise at my door. It appeared like the fall of my door. I suppose it waked me. About the time I was getting out of bed I heard some matches striking, and I saw they were disguised men. They seized on to me by my arms and took me out of doors.

They took me out into the big road, which is about thirty yards, and started west into the road; went some fifty yards and they turned back and went into the other end of the road, took me about a hundred yards from my house, I reckon, and there was a tree standing right over the fence. The panel of the fence was against the tree, and they set me right over in the field and put my arms around the tree and a man stood over in the roadside and held me around the tree till they whipped me.

Q. Go on and tell what they did to you.

A. They whipped me severely. At times I didn't understand anything. I think I fainted away at times. I reckon from the way I was whipped, bruised and everything, that they must have given me a hundred lashes or more. I didn't get over it for a month or two.

Q. What clothing did you have on when they whipped you?

A. I had on my shirt and drawers.

Q. Did they whip you over your shirt?

A. No, sir, they tucked my shirt up and put it through the collar here.

Q. Why didn't you tell that without my asking you?

A. Well, I didn't think of it.

Q. Then they whipped you on your bare back?

A. Yes, sir; then they let me loose from around the tree, put me astraddle of the fence and held me there, and whipped my legs.

Q. State whether you were badly bruised.

A. Well, I don't think I could have put my three fingers down on a place but what was bruised black.

Q. How far on your person did they extend?

A. It was from my shoulders here clean down to my feet.

Q. What did they whip you for?

A. Well, they said they whipped me—they said I had shut my wife up in the smoke house and whipped her.

Q. Had you done that?

A. I had not.

Q. I ask you if you did not try to establish your wife and daughters in a whore-house, and you and your wife quarrel about it?

A. No, sir

...

ALPHONSO GERRINGER *colored*

Q. State whether anything was done to you in Alamance County, or not.

A. Well, I was going to a debate one night with my cousin, and met up with two men. Before we got there, I heard somebody halloa out, not natural, and I told him I heard somebody that did not halloa out natural—What does that mean? He said he didn't know.

Q. State what sort of a noise you heard.

A. Well, it didn't appear to be a natural voice at all. We went on a little further, and I heard it again. He said it was some of them boys over there at the school house holloaing—they were about broke up. He said, "Let's hurry, or they will be gone before we get there." I went on a little further, and I saw two disguised men, or they appeared like men—I didn't know. They had white gowns on and horns about as big as my arm. They came out of the bushes right so, and throwed their hands up.

Q. Tell how they looked.

A. Well, they were disguised men—had these white gowns on and horns about as big as my arm. We were in a big road—Bill goes right up the big road, mind you, and me after him. Well, they caught me, and he got away; but after they caught me, I say, "Cousin Bill, come here," twice or three times, I don't recollect. I tell the truth about it. He says, "I can't." He went on a little farther, and I called him again. He says, "I can't." Well, they took me just about a quarter of a mile before they stopped with me. I says, "Friends, what have you got me here for, I haven't done you any harm nor any other man at all?"

Well, they said they were going to take me down here in this piece of woods. I went along with them. If they had asked me to go anywhere I would have went. When I got down there, they said they were going to kill me, to hang me.

They had a wythe. There had been a big tree cut down in time, and there is a hickory; there is a wythe that grows out as long as my arm. I fell down. One of them raised me up and pulled the wythe around my neck and let me down—

Q. State whether it hurt you or not?

A. No, sir, it didn't hurt me. I concluded that they took me along just to bother me.

Q. You needn't tell anything you concluded. Just tell what was done.

A. Well, they hung me up and told me that I had to pray—that they were going to kill me. Well, I didn't know what they were going to do—didn't know what sort of men they were.

Q. What did you do?

A. I got down and prayed. [*laughter*] Well, they put me up again and let me down, and they told me I had to run. Then you had better seen me running—I told my legs to save my body if they could, and I didn't see any more of them at all. [*great merriment*]

The CHIEF JUSTICE. Don't try to be funny. Just tell the truth.

A. Well, that's it. Yes, the last I saw of them.

Q. How many of them were there?

A. There wasn't but two. They looked like two men—I don't know whether they were or not. I ain't used to the critters. [*laughter*]

Q. Do you know what they did it for?

A. No, sir, I did not.

Q. Didn't you know that they did it because you had insulted some old lady, or say something vulgar to her?

A. No, sir; I heard of this after this deed was done, but I never did upon my honor—never made a raid upon an old woman. [*laughter*]

...

SAMUEL ALLEN *colored, 44 &*
ABI ALLEN *his wife*

Q. What is your occupation?

A. Well, sir, I am a shoemaker.

Q. State whether you have ever been visited by disguised men and if so what they did.

A. Yes, sir. They came first and struck against the door with a club, and kind of drove against it and burst it open. Then they commenced calling to open the door. I was not asleep. I acted if I was asleep, and when they tried to open the door I said, "It is a late hour, what do you want?"

They said, "Get up, get up, why don't you get up?" several times.

My wife said not to do so. After a while, I proceeded to the door and opened it and they commenced to try and burst open the door with a stone and other instruments of wood and some of them shot against the door and the ball struck a nail and turned off and I could see it the next morning. They bursted a hole through the door and then they commenced to call to open the door.

I then went and opened the door and they said, "Why did not you open the door before?"

I said, "My wife wasn't willing and therefore I delayed."

They said, "Come out here."

I said, "What do you want of me?"

One of them said, "The sooner you come out the better it will be for you." Another said, "Shoot him,"–and he presented a pistol, but he sort of gave way, and another said, "No, no!"

I said, "Gentlemen, you said you wanted to talk with me, what have you to say? I am ready to hear anything you have got to say, if you want to talk with me."

They said, "Come out here, come out here."

I said, "I shall not do it." I turned around and went back expecting they would make a rush on me and take me by force from my home. I went and got a sabre that I had at the end of the bed and went back to the door and there was one of them standing near the door and I took that sabre and I thrust it at him with all my vengeance—I am sure I did. Then I slapped the door right to and commenced putting up my fortifications.

Q. Your what?

A. My fortifications. My door had fortifications to fasten it again. Then they said, "Let us go and burn up the house."

As soon as I got my fortifications up I turned and went through a little window that led into the kitchen of my home, which is weather-boarded, and when I got in there and discovered that they were striking matches and getting rags and other things to make a flame, the thought struck me that they would surely burn up the house for the purpose of getting me out. I turned round and went back through the window into the other house and got back and went out of the east door and looked to see if there was any of them there. Then I jumped out and run a little beyond the house.

When they saw me they said, "Shoot him—shoot him— shoot him," and they shot after me, and they holload "Catch him—catch him—catch him," and they ran after me for about a hundred and fifty yards, as near as I can guess and then they stopped and I was very glad they did, for I was tired myself. Then I went on, and I saw no more of them that night.

The second time they were there I wasn't at home. I was coming from Greensboro' to Yanceyville.

Q. That is the only time you saw them?

A. That is the only time they ever attacked me.

Q. You saw them the first time they passed in the road?

A. Yes, sir.

Q. You did nothing that night?

A. No, sir.

Q. Did they make any noises?

A. Oh, screaming.

Q. How were they disguised?

A. In white—the moon was up then. I could see nothing but white—you know I did not attempt to count them.

Q. What took place the next morning?

A. The next morning when I got back home there lay a club about four feet long, which was not shown at all that night when they were talking to me at the door. I saw nothing but their pistols and this weapon, as I told you.

Q. How many pistols did you see?

A. It seemed like the most of them had something. But I saw no stick or hickory. The next morning there were three— one of them I could sit here and reach that gentleman with [*referring to Mr. Merrimon, counsel for the managers*]. It was as thick as my thumb at the big end of it, a regular ox driver, and the other two were almost four feet long, I think about the size of my finger, like hickory switches, that lay out there near the house by the door or the end of the chimney.

Q. Where did you stay that night?

A. I stayed out in the woods, about three quarters of a mile from home.

Q. Are you living in the county of Caswell?

A. Oh no, sir.

Q. When did you leave?

A. I left there on the 13th, I think—on the 15th I believe, of May.

Q. How long after this visit?

A. Well, I know that was Monday night my house was attacked—the next Friday night it was attacked for the second time. I got home Saturday evening by dusk and dark, and I left Sunday morning to leave that country.

Q. What caused you to leave?

A. Well, from what I understood they said, and what they did, and the raid that they had made, by persons that were there, and others who lived in the upper end of the lot that they made get up and come down amongst them to my house, and told them what to tell me—so he said—why I would not risk my life there at all, for my belief was that the decree was to kill me, night or day, just when the opportunity afforded.

Q. Did you see the body of Robin Jacobs?

A. No, sir, that was taken about Saturday before I reached home—Saturday in the day sometime.

Q. Why didn't you attempt to prosecute them?

A. I was afraid of my life—I was afraid after this second raid to pass anywhere in the day time on any business it made no odds what.

Q. What did you do when you reached Caswell?

A. I went to Yanceyville and delivered a message to Mr. Stephens that was given to me by my wife. I got home on Saturday. She told me on Sunday morning of a message that a certain lady had delivered her for me to carry to Mr. Stephens.

Q. How long was that before the murder of Stephens?

A. I don't think that it was much over a week; it might have been over two weeks.

Q. Where did you go from Yanceyville?

A. I went from Yanceyville to Greensboro'—took the cars at Greensboro'.

Q. Where did you go from Greensboro'?

A. I came from Greensboro' to this place.

Q. What did you do when you got to Raleigh?

A. When I got to Raleigh I went to the governor and informed him of the condition of that county and my condition. I had done that one time before—I did that the first time they were seen in that neighborhood.

Q. When was that?

A. That was in February.

Q. Tell all you told the governor.

A. Well, I cannot tell you, I don't reckon, all I told him. But I will tell you what I can. I told him that myself and the colored people of my county, as a general thing, to my knowledge, were in the terror—in a state of terror and it was their request that there should be protection sent there for them—myself as one having been run off from all I possessed in the world, the dangers to which I was exposed, and that if there could be any such thing as giving us protection, I wanted him to do it. If he would do nothing more, if he would only furnish men to go over with me to guard me while I should get away with my things, for I knew it would endanger me to go to that county by myself.

Q. I understand you to say you stated to him that the civil laws could not protect you there at all?

A. Oh! No, sir, no protection whatever, not a bit, it was not worth a cent, of course; it was not worth a cent. All the law that could be, would be worth nothing, that is the civil law.

ABI ALLEN *colored, also testified about these events.*

Q. I want you to tell all you know about disguised persons coming to your house, all that they said, and all you know about it.

A. Well, the first time I saw them they was somewhere in February, about the 13th I think. They passed there, and they didn't make any stop; they just passed on. We heard the racket, and we went out and saw them pass on.

Q. Now go to the second time. We don't care so much about the first time.

A. The second time they came we were in bed. I heard a rush, the dog gave a bark, and someone rushed against the door pelting at the door and calling Sam Allen. I don't know particularly that they said him but calling to "Open the door, open the door." Well, he didn't reply to them you know, and in a few minutes they called again, "Open the door." Well, I told him not to answer, and upon that they commenced shouting and pelting against the door with a pole and rock, and other instruments until they punched a hole through the door. Directly he got up and he went to the door. I told him not to go before the door, they might shoot him. We steps to the window about the door, and I raised the curtain, and looked out there. They were standing right in the yard saying, "Open the door." He opened the door and when he opened the door he went into the door, and I goes and stands in the door by his side. They talked to him, and they told him to come out, and asked why he didn't open the door when they told him. Well, he said because his wife was not willing. Said I to them, "What are you here for—what business have you got that you come at this time of night—this is no time of night to come to a man's house at the dead hour of night to roust him out of his sleep."

Well, one of them said, "The least you say the better for you," and he presented a pistol, and said he would shoot me.

They then gave back and one of them said shoot him. They might have presented a pistol at him. They went on and told him to "Come out here."

Well, he says, "You told me to open the door, you wanted to talk with me—here I am to hear what you have got to say."

They said, "Will you come out here to us?" They stood around in the yard and said, "Come out here to us."

Well, he turned off and says, "I shan't do it" and turns around, when he turns around one of them threatens to shoot. I sort of steps around to t'other side of him to the door, and takes hold of the edge of the door, and pulls, and he came around by me, and passed on to the head of the bed. I didn't look back to see where he was going, but I slammed the door to as soon as he comes out of the door, and when I slammed the door so, there was one standing by the side of the house on my right side, he jumped up and pushed the door open and it struck me short here, which hurt me very bad for some days, and I pushed against the door trying to push it to, and he pushes against me rather hard. We didn't get the door to right smart. The first thing I knew my husband came by me with a sword in his hand, or a sabre, whatever they call it, and thrust him out of the door with his sabre, and when he thrust him he pitched away out into the yard sideways, and from that when he thrust him out there some of the rest held up their hands, and made sort of screaming. He never said anything, but as soon as my husband slammed the door to I sort of steps to the window close by, and there he lay right by the road before the west door right out to the big road.

Well, he was fixing his door. Directly he fixed it, he went right through between the beds. We entered into the kitchen, and when we entered in he goes through with me. I says to him, "You had better not come in here." When I got in there I saw them setting the kitchen part next to the window afire. I saw the matches blaze, and I got through there, and goes to the door. He comes and takes away the prop against the door, and said I, "You had better not come out here." I said, "I will try to save the house," and I goes to the door and open it, and said I, "Gentlemen, do please don't burn up my house." Well, he turned back. I never knowed when he left, but he went out from me, and I didn't seem him no more that night. I pled for the house, I begged them not to burn it, for said I, "The leather in here will break the neighbors up in the way of leather and shoes."

"Well," said they, "What do you take in work for?"

"Well," said I, "That is the way we live."

From that they went on a few minutes. I heard some of them say, "Yonder he goes, yonder he goes, shoot him, shoot him."

I still stood in the door, and begged them to tell me what he had done. Said I, "Gentlemen, tell me if you please what Sam Allen has done—what are you after?"

They would not tell me what they wanted of him. I again plead with them not to burn the house, and told them I didn't know a thing he had done. Well they would not tell me what he had done, but just said they were going to have him.

They ran after him a piece, I don't know how far, because I didn't see them, but they came back. I saw them come back down through the garden, one in particular. He comes up in the yard, and says to me—I was standing in the door—said he, "What did you let him get out for?"

Said I, "I could not help it."

"Well," he says, "we intend to have him on the risk of our lives, and I want you to tell him we intend to hang him away up yonder." Said he, "You tell him when he comes back that he belongs to us and the devil." And upon that they began to move off to the field, where this one was hurt I guess for he went down on the road. They began to go off a few at a time, until they all went off till you may have seen half a dozen or more in the yard. They kept lighting, you know, trying to burn the house, and I kept begging them not to burn it. At last some of them lit a rag or something and throwed it on me and every once in a while they threatened to shoot me. Well this one that came down through the garden, he came up to me and said, "I know you have let him out." Some of them said, "Shoot her," and he took out a pistol and throwed it up and struck me, and the blow glanced down. It hurt me for several days, but they didn't shoot nary time. There was one staid behind back in the yard and he talked to me after these were all gone down to the house. He had a lantern in hand all the time—it was sitting in the yard burning. He said to me when they were all gone, said he, "If you ain't every one gone from here by to-morrow night"—that was Monday night—"if you ain't every one of you gone from here by Tuesday night we intend to come another night and kill every one of you and burn every house on the premises." We still staid on in the day time for a week afterwards.

Q. Go on to the night Robin Jacobs was there.

A. I was not at home that night. I staid at home until ten o'clock, and this young man that boarded at my house came and persuaded me to leave. I went to a neighbor's house and staid there. Betwixt midnight and the day I was awakened by the report of a gun very loud. I wasn't quite asleep, but it waked me up so that I jumped up and run out of doors and right over towards my house. I never did in all my lifetime hear such a racket. It seemed the old field, plantation and everything about there was just in a yelp like geese. It seemed like there was something like two or three hundred making a fuss. In that old field it seemed like and that six acre lot was covered with men halloaing and yelling. The old man that I staid with, who was something like seventy years old said he never heard such a to do in his life. I expected every minute to see a flame at my house and I takes the two boys there and tries to get to where I could see them. I found they were making towards the road—they were coming towards the big road, and I waited until they made it over the hill down towards the road and they seemed to cease to make the racket.

Q. What year—was it last year or when?

A. It was last May. They were there on Monday night and the next Friday night they came back.

Q. When did you leave there?

A. I left there in the last of May, I think.

Q. What did you leave there for?

A. I left because I was afraid of the Kuklux; my husband was gone for two weeks. He left me there to take care of the things. I never staid in my house a night—I laid out when I didn't stay in the neighboring houses for two weeks, and I couldn't stand it any longer so I had to come away.

Q. You laid out in the woods a good deal of the time?

A. Yes, sir, staid in thickets and old fields.

Q. How many children did you have with you?

A. I had one. I had to carry it with me.

Q. How old is he?

A. Eight years old coming nine.

JOSEPH MEBANE *colored, also testified about this event.*

Q. State whether or not you have been interfered with by men in disguise and if so when?

A. I was teaching school in Caswell County. I boarded at Mr. Allen's. I taught school about fifty yards from his house on the main big road. In February, the last clause of it, if I mistake not, was the first of my knowing of these disguised men. They passed by Mr. Allen's house.

Q. How many were there?

A. They looked to be about twenty-five or thirty, about that—that is my estimation about it.

Q. What did they do?

A. They did not do anything only passed there and they halloaed and went on.

Q. Halloaed how?

A. They holloaed in a peculiar way. I can't change my voice, like they changed theirs.

Q. What time was that?

A. That was the last of February, if I mistake not. In May I saw them again a second time when they attacked Mr. Allen.

Q. What time was that?

A. It was something about twelve o'clock I heard the dog barking. It seemed as if they made a rush against the door, and battering against it. They commenced halloaing towards the door, but Allen did not open the door as they requested. They said, "Open the door, we don't want to hurt you," but he didn't open the door, and they commenced battering the door again with a pole sixteen feet long, and a very large rock which they threw against the door and battered a hole through the door, and they began shooting through it.

Q. What else took place?

A. Then they commanded Mr. Allen to open the door, that they would not hurt him, but open the door he must. After that he got up and opened the door, and they asked him why he did not open the door when they told him. He said that his wife was not willing he should open the door, and he delayed it. He was then standing in the door and they said, "Come out here to us"; he said, "I shall not do it"; and he turned right around and stepped back in the house, and got a sabre there, expecting that they would rush upon him, and he returned with the sabre, and one of these disguised men was standing in the door, and he thrust that sword at him, and after that he closed the door. Then they said, "We will set the house on fire." It was a double house with a kitchen, which was connected with the big house by a weather boarding. They went to the south corner and set it on fire. He closed the door after he thrust the sabre at this disguised man, and they had gone to the south end of the house to set it on fire. They were striking matches. Then his wife went I suppose in the kitchen from the big house and begged them not to set it on fire.

Q. You could hear her?

A. Yes, sir. Then Mr. Allen he opened the back door and ran off, and as they discovered him they halloaed, "Shoot at him," and they ran after him, I suppose about two hundred and fifty yards, and shot at him.

Q. Did they catch him?

A. No, sir, they didn't succeed in catching him. After they returned I heard them say, "We intend to have revenge." They asked his wife where was that teacher—that they wanted him. She replied that he had gone home with some of the children from school.

Q. By the teacher, they meant you?

A. Yes, sir, I was a teacher there at the time. I made myself quite still. I didn't make any noise at all. [*laughter*] One of the men said it was not so, that he saw me in the yard that evening just at dark.

Q. You laid very low?

A. Yes, sir, I kept very quiet. After that I suppose they left. They went off a piece, and she could hear them saying, "Let us go back—"

Mr. GRAHAM. You need not state what she heard.

The WITNESS. At last after they went off she says—

Q. Never mind what she said—you need not tell anything but what you heard yourself.

A. Well, they went off.

CHIEF JUSTICE. Did they come back?

A. No, sir. She told me to go, that they were coming back, and I jerked on my pants, and I ran off and laid out that night. That was on Monday night, the ninth of May. I taught school that week, then on Friday night after twelve o'clock or one o'clock, I and four other men were there. We stayed up every night after that first time they visited me, and went in the woods. We were afraid to stay in the house. I taught my school in the day, and would stay out in the woods at night. On the Friday night four other men came to stay up with me—to keep company with Allen's wife and myself. We didn't stay in the house, but we went off in the woods, and stayed there till about one o'clock, when some of the men suggested, "They will not be here, let us go to the house," and we went to the house, and built up a little fire.

But my feelings would not allow me to stay in the house, for I believed that they would be there, and I told them so. Well, something after one o'clock, I was standing by the door, and I looked up the road about three hundred yards and I saw a body—something white moving. I stepped into the house and said, "Men, the Kuklux are coming."

They went to the door and looked, and they said, "No, it was the moon shining against the trees," and they went back and sat down.

Presently I saw them coming on the road on horseback, and I said, "Men, let us get out, here they are—the Kuklux," and myself and three other men rushed out over the big road, but Robin Jacobs turned round the corner of the house. I said, "Uncle Jacob, come along." But I never heard him say anything as he went on. We got out of the way and Robin Jacobs went the contrary way altogether.

Q. When did you see him next?

A. The next morning. I saw him lying about one hundred fifty yards from Samuel Allen's house, dead. I saw him the next morning with a very large hole in his shoulder. It looked very much as if he had been shot. I heard the report of a gun.

Q. He was dead?

A. Yes, sir, he was a dead man.

Q. Did you see how these men were disguised?

A. Yes, sir, in white—something like gowns, and they had horns on them.

Q. Did you see them the last night you spoke of?

A. Yes, sir, I saw them every night.

Q. How many do you think there were that night?

A. I can only suggest that I saw them coming at a distance, and I didn't have time to look to see how many. There appeared to be two hundred or three hundred.

Q. How long did you remain there?

A. The next morning I left the county—Saturday morning.

Mr. GRAHAM: You were teaching at a public school?

A. No, an entered school.

Q. Mr. Ashley was superintendent of public schools in this state.

A. I don't know whether you call it a public school or not.

Q. Don't you know that Mr. Jacob Dick was commissioner of teachers in the county of Caswell?

A. Not that I know of.

Q. You were never sent to him?

A. Mr. Ashley paid me $10 for rent for the school, if I mistake not.

Q. It was for the support of the school in some way—it was a contribution of $10 by the superintendent of public schools for that school?

A. He said for rent, but they could pay it to the school teacher if necessary.

The CHIEF JUSTICE. How does this inquiry become important?

Mr. GRAHAM, prosecution. I think it is important to know something in reference to the circumstances under which this witness was there. I am endeavoring to show he was teaching a public school without any authority of law.

Mr. BOYDEN, defense. Mr. Chief Justice, I think it is very competent to show that the witness was not licensed to teach a school, and consequently the Kuklux had a right to go and shoot him.

Mr. MERRIMON, prosecution. Mr. Chief Justice, the examination is competent to show that this witness was a surreptitious person, with a view to impeach him in that way, if we can do so.

Mr. GRAHAM. He claims to be a public character.

The CHIEF JUSTICE. His only claim is getting $10 from Mr. Ashley, so far as the presiding officer can see.

Q. You say that you were living at Allen's?
A. Yes, sir.

Q. Sam Allen's?
A. Yes, sir.

Q. You say that when he came to the house he thrust at one of them with a sword?

A. Yes, sir.

Q. Did he not stick the sword into him?

A. I think he stuck it into him.

Q. What else did he tell you at the time he did—did he not say that he stuck it into him so far that he had hard work to pull it out?

A. Allen's reply that he made was that he—

Q. Didn't he say that he could hardly pull it out?

A. Yes, sir, it was pretty hard to get it out.

Q. Did the man fall on that occasion—did you find him?

A. I don't know whether he fell off from the steps—I did not see him after he got out.

Q. Didn't Allen say the sword went through him?

A. He did not say whether it went through him or not.

Q. You didn't take the man up afterwards and bury him?

A. No, sir, he was taken off that night I suppose.

Q. That was on the occasion of their first visit?

A. No, sir, that was the second visit. That was the first time they attacked us.

WESLEY MITCHELL *colored, 24, also testified about this event.*

Q. State whether or not disguised men ever visited you?

A. Yes, sir. The first time they came along was about February, I think. I just saw them passing in the road that time I heard them coming; I heard a dreadful noise up the road. I run out of the house and saw them coming. I went back and shut the front door, came out of the back door, and they didn't come to the door. Then I went back and opened both doors and stood in the door till they passed.

Q. How many do you think they were?

A. Well, I think there were about twenty or twenty-five—maybe more than that.

Q. Did they make any noise?

A. Yes, sir, they made a dreadful noise.

Q. What sort of noise?

A. They made a noise like geese and some like dogs; some were going one way and some another; some were squalling; and I can't tell what sort of noise they were all making.

Q. When did you see them next?

A. The next time I saw them was the 9th of May.

Q. State what happened then.

A. Well, I saw them at Sam Allen's house, and they woke me up by bumping at his door. I raised up—I was in bed—and there was a little crack right opposite my house, next to his house; and I got up and peeped through the crack. I saw his yard looked white with disguised men. I knew what they were as soon as I saw them, but I just stood up on the bed and looked at them and heard them bumping and bumping at his door. I got up and thought I would go out, and then I thought they may come to my house. I got up and again stood on the bed, and I heard them say, "You come out here," and I heard them tell him to open the door. I could hear them talking.

Q. Was that all at Allen's house?

A. That was all done at Allen's house. The next I heard was the men at Allen's said, "Shoot him! shoot him! shoot him!" And I saw him running. I heard them talking to his wife, and heard her talking to them, but what they said I could not know. So they went off that night and that is all I know about it. The next time they came back was on a Friday night. I was asleep when they came, I reckon it was about one o'clock and there was a window right at my house where I had had a bench where I shoemaked. I saw them passing by and heard the talking as plain as I am talking, and it scared me because I hadn't rested any in the house since they came there on Monday night. I staid in the house, but I never slept much—I was up and down all night long; I expected them to come back again, and I lay down very little in the night. I lay down I reckon about twelve o'clock. I reckon I had just got sound asleep though and they woke me up talking, and I jumped upon the floor. I could tell that they altered their voices, and then I went to the bed again, and got upon the bed again, and stood and looked down towards Allen's house and the yard was as thick with them as they could lie—about an acre of ground, I reckon, betwixt the road and his house, and it looked as though it was thick with them.

Q. An acre of ground looked like it was thick with them?

A. Yes, sir, about that much betwixt his house and the road, I reckon. It appeared to me like there was more than that but it was thick with them.

Q. Were they in disguise?

A. Yes, sir, the moon shone as bright as day, and I could see the red tassils on their heads, but I couldn't see anything about their eyes until they came to my house. I will tell you about that directly. [*laughter*]

Q. Go on?

A. Six of them, when I was standing up there, went from my house down to Allen's, and twelve of them came back. When they came back, some were by the back door and some at the front door knocking and asking—"Open the door." I never replied to them till they said the same to me three or four times.

Well, I got up after a while and opened the door. No—I got up, and they said to me, "Go to the front door; don't come to this door." I went to the front door and I opened the door and they made their obeisance to me. [*laughter*] They asked me, "Do you see us?"

I told them I did.

They said, "Who have you got here?"

Said I, "I am here."

Said they, "Where is Allen?"

Said I, "I don't know anything about him."

Said they, "Have you got anybody here?"

Said I, "I haven't got anybody here but myself and my brother George and a little boy"—just so. They stood there a while and said, "Where is that little boy?"

I said, "He is in bed."

They said, "Call him up"—they wanted to see him.

I called him up, and they asked him what he was doing there, and he said he was doing nothing only he was come to stay with his uncle Wesley to keep him company.

Mr. BOYDEN, defense. What was that? I did not hear.

A. This little boy told the Kuklux that I got him to come and stay with me. They asked me what he was doing there, and I told them that I had nobody to stay there with me, that I had lost my wife and wanted somebody to keep me company and I got this little boy to come and stay with me. They then asked me again where was Allen, and I told them, "I don't know anything about Allen,"—just so. Then they asked me if I were scared.

I told them I were.

They said, "You don't look like you are scared."

I told them I were, just so.

Then they told me to call my brother, and I called him down, and they asked him where was Allen. He told them he didn't know anything about Allen. He said he worked over to Mr. Reed's.

Then they said to me, "Come on, you and your brother have got [Allen] to find."

"Well," said I, "let me get my breeches and put them on."

"No," said he, "we've been to hell many a time in our drawers, and you can go too,"—just so. I walked out of the house and shut the door, and they said, "Little boy, you can stay there: there ain't nobody going to hurt you." They carried me on down there—me and my brother George, and got over the fence there at the garden and stopped. Said they, "You have got to find him tonight."

"Well," said we, "we don't know whether he is there or not."

"Well," said they, "the door is open."

"Well," said I, "of course he cannot be there if the door is open." We went in there and there was nobody at his house.

"Well," said he, "you have got to find him to-night. If you don't we will carry you in the woods and swing you to a limb,"—just so.

After a while one of them said, "Do you know any of us?"

I told him I did not.

Said he, "You are sure you don't know any of us?" He had a pistol up at my breast, said he, "G-d d--n you, tell the truth now, do you know any of us?"

"No," said I, "I don't know any of you, how could I know you men disguised in that way?"

Well, he stood there a while. Now, said he, "Look here, let me tell you if you don't know any of us; don't you have anything to do with the Kuklux, nor meddle with them and we will have nothing to do with you."

I told him I would not. I asked them could I go in and make up a fire, they said yes, make up a fire and shut the door. I shut the door and that is the last I know of them. They went on then up towards old man Paylor's.

Q. Did you know Robin Jacobs?

A. Yes, sir, he was my wife's uncle.

Q. Did he hold any office?

A. No, sir, he was nothing but a farming man.

Q. Did you see his body after he was killed?

A. I did.

Q. Just describe in what manner he was killed.

A. The next morning when I got up, I discovered a man, I did not go quite to him but I went to the fence and I see'd then—

Q. Was that the place where you had seen the Kuklux the night before?

A. Yes, sir, betwixt my house and old man John Paylor's. I just turned up the fence and called old man Paylor—an old man that lived t'other side of my house.

Q. A colored man?

A. Yes, sir, and I told him here is old Uncle Robin Jacobs near about dead.

Q. State what you saw.

A. That is all I saw. After I told him, I went over to the fence and halloaed to him and he ketched hold of my hand, he seemed to try to say something to me, but he could not say it and I just turned off from him and saw him no more.

Q. What was done with him?

A. He was shot here betwixt the fore shoulders.

Q. Betwixt the fore shoulders? [*laughter*]

A. I mean betwixt the shoulders—I make mistakes sometimes. [*laughter*]

Q. Was he dead?

A. He just barely had breath in him.

Q. Did you see any blood on him?

A. Yes, sir, he was bloody all over his side here, on his shoulders and all around his neck here, and I asked John Paylor to examine him and see where he was shot, in order that I might know.

Q. Was Allen stirring up strife between the whites and blacks, and inciting the blacks to burn barns?

A. No, sir.

Q. Wasn't he a very odious man in that neighborhood?

A. Yes, sir.

Mr. BOYDEN, defense. The witness does not know what "odious" means.

Q. Do you know what "odious" means?

A. No, sir, I don't know.

Q. Well, I mean this: Wasn't he a very objectionable man to people there? Didn't they hate him—didn't everybody hate him?

A. No, sir, they didn't. People liked him very well—if that is what you want.

Q. He had the reputation of being a good man?

A. Why of course. Allen has been as popular a man among white and black there as I know of. He was called about the best shoemaker that there was there, and everybody liked him. [*laughter*]

...

JOHN WALTER STEPHENS *white, 35*

John Stephens was serving in the North Carolina Senate when he was assassinated by Kuklux in the basement of the Caswell County court house on a Saturday afternoon, May 13, 1870, while a Democratic party convention continued in the court room above. William Stephens started searching for his brother about 4 p.m. that afternoon; he and his younger brother were unable to find Sen. Stephens and spent the night in the court house, with "a cordon of guards all around." On Sunday morning, they found their brother "directly after light."

William Stephens testified:

Q. What position was he in—in the room?

A. Well, there had been some wood put in there and cut up about three or four feet along for a fire-place, and was piled across the north end of the room. There seemed to be a gap in the room. He was sitting in the gap in the wood, and his head was thrown back into the wood.

Q. Did you notice the rope around his neck?

A. Yes, sir. The rope was drawn very tight around his neck—buried in the neck.

Q. State what you saw of blood.

A. Well, there was right smart of blood in there on the wood and trash—the chips—and on the wall.

Q. How did that on the wall appear to be there—from a jet of blood?

A. Yes, sir; it looked as though it jetted there.

— from the *New York Times*

Senator Stephens Murdered by Kuklux in N. Carolina

RALEIGH, N. C. Feb. 25 [1871] Mr. Bowman, Republican, related from the sworn evidence of one of the parties present the particulars of the murder of Senator John W. Stephens, of Caswell, which occurred in [May] 1870; and that warrants had been issued for the guilty parties.

He stated that a public Democratic meeting was in progress in the court-house at Yanceyville, the county seat of Caswell; that Stephens was in attendance on that meeting; that a prominent Democrat of Caswell approached Stephens with a smile, and asked him to go down-stairs with him. Stephens assented, and they went into a room formerly occupied by the Clerk of the Court of Equity; that as soon as they entered the room the door was locked; that there were in the room eight white men and one negro. Stephens was surprised to find the room full of men, and was struck with horror when a rope, fixed as a lasso, was thrown over his neck from behind, and he was told by the spokesman of the Kuklux crowd that he must renounce his Republican principles. He replied that he believed they were right, and that the Republic would prosper if they were carried out; that he could not leave the country and State, because his all was there; that the colored people looked upon him as a leader, that they depended on him, and that he could not desert them.

Stephens was then told that he must die. He then asked to be allowed to take a last look from the window of the office, at his home and any of his family that might be in view.

The request was granted, and when Stephens stepped to the window he beheld his little home and his two little children playing in front of his house.

He was then thrown down on a table, two of the Kuklux holding his arms. The rope was ordered to be drawn tighter, and the negro was ordered to get a bucket to catch the blood. This done, one of the crowd severed the jugular vein, the negro caught the blood in the bucket, and Stephens was dead. His body was laid on a pile of wood in the room, and the murderers went up-stairs, took part in the meeting, and stamped and applauded Democratic speeches.

ADDITIONAL CITIZENS TERRORIZED BY KUKLUX IN & NEAR ALAMANCE COUNTY

Eleven citizens terrorized by Kuklux in Alamance & Caswell counties, as revealed in the Holden impeachment trial.

Lewis Baines *white*
Porter Dixon *colored*
a man named Ham *colored*
a man named Hightower *colored*
Daniel Isley *colored*
Jerry Lee *colored*
Norfolk Malone *colored*
Alson Shoe *white*
Thomas Siddell *white, 65*
Nathan Trollinger *colored, 65*
Ivison Warren *colored*

Forty-eight citizens terrorized by Kuklux in Alamance County, 1868–1871, as revealed in the *Report on the Alleged Outrages in the Southern States*, by the Select Committee of the United States Senate, March 10, 1871. This list does not include citizens whose testimony was recorded in the Holden impeachment trial.

Harvey Albright *colored, whipped*

Moses Albright *colored, whipped*

John Albright *colored, whipped*

William R. Albright *white, threatened*

Squire Alston & his wife *colored. Justice of the Peace P. R. Harden testified to the U.S. Senate: "Quite a number of them went to his house. When they broke open the door and got into the house, Alston's wife picked up an ax and struck at one of the party, and cut his head nearly open. It was thought for a while that he would certainly die from the effects of the wound. The party got into a general wrangle or fight, and I do not think they got the negro out so as to give him a real whipping; but the thing was given up on account of the fight they got into there."*

N.A. Badham *visited by "seventy-five disguised persons" who "halted, and formed in front" of his home, "frightened his family, and threatened and insulted him."*

John Bass *colored, whipped*

Harry Cain *his house shot up*

Henderson Coble *colored, whipped*

Levi Dickey *colored. Failing to find him, the marauding party "choked his wife in a most inhumane manner."*

Arch. Duke *colored, whipped*
Lizzie Elmore *white, whipped & run off*
Anthony Foster *white, 80, whipped & kicked "until life was nearly extinct"*
Amos Forsehea *colored, whipped*
John Foust *colored, whipped*
Thomas Foust *colored, whipped*
Matilda Foust *colored, whipped*
Rachel Foust *colored, whipped*
Mrs. Foy & daughter *white, thrown from their home and "both of them badly beaten and maltreated"*
Monroe [Michael?] Freeland *colored, whipped*
William [Cyrus?] Guy *colored, whipped "and afterwards hung—he was hung in Orange"*
Peter R. Harden *white, along with* **N.A. Badham,** *threatened with punishment "unless they ceased to prosecute Kuklux"; soon after Outlaw's lynching, one local plan was "that Peter Harden would go up in a few days—the boys were bent on killing him."*
Alfred Hartwell *colored, whipped*
Duncan Hazel *colored, whipped*
William Hornaday *white, "shot at in his own house, very nearly killing his wife."*
Lindsay Kinnery *colored, whipped*
John Linins *white, whipped & run off*
James Long *colored, whipped & forced to flee county*
John Morrow *colored school teacher, "severely scourged"*
Harrison Mulkins *whipped severely*
Thomas Norwood *sentenced to be drowned.* [*sentence was not carried out*]
William Overman *colored, house broken up*
Alvis Pichard *white, whipped & run off*
John Piles *colored, his house burned down*
Hamilton Puryear

Murphy Reeves *white, shot*
Oliver Shaffer *colored, whipped*
Senator T. M. Shoffner *forced to flee county for safety*
William Shoffner *white, 17, whipped*
Clay Thompson *colored, whipped*
Alfred White *colored, whipped*
Linneaus White *colored*
Don Worth *colored, whipped*
Jonathan Zachray

The U.S. Senate report lists only three persons as having been terrorized by KuKlux in Caswell County: **Samuel Allen**, whose testimony is recounted in this book, and a person named **Jones**; and it mistakenly reports that **Senator John Stephens**, who was murdered in the basement of the Caswell County court house, was shot and survived.

61 Citizens Terrorized by Kuklux in & near Alamance County, North Carolina,
1868–1870, as told in their own words & attested by others in the
official transcript of the impeachment trial of Governor William W. Holden

Pre-production by **Stanton Blakeslee**
Typesetting by Eva Roberts using **Adobe Caslon Pro**

Art Direction and Design by **Eva Roberts**
Cover design by **Stanton Blakeslee**

ISBN 978-0-9842102-5-1

about the editor
Alex Albright grew up in Alamance County and graduated from Graham High School in 1969. His 2013 book, *The Forgotten First: B-1 and the Integration of the Modern Navy*, was also designed by Eva Roberts. He and his wife, Elizabeth, live in Fountain, NC.

about the designer
Eva Roberts first lived in North Carolina in 1956; she earned a Master of Product Design in 1976 from NC State University School of Design. She lives in Raleigh close to her daughters. Throughout her career she has welcomed opportunities to work with Alex Albright.

published by
R.A. Fountain
PO Box 44
Fountain, NC 27829

www.rafountain.com